LEADING FOR GROWTH

JB JOSSEY-BASS

LEADING FOR GROWTH

How Umpqua Bank Got Cool and Created a Culture of Greatness

Ray Davis with Alan Shrader

BICENTENNIAL
1807
WILEY
2007
BICENTENNIAL

John Wiley & Sons, Inc.

Published by Jossey-Bass
A Wiley Imprint
989 Market Street, San Francisco, CA 94103-1741 www.josseybass.com

Jossey-Bass books and products are available through most bookstores. To contact Jossey-Bass directly
call our Customer Care Department within the U.S. at 800-956-7739, outside the U.S. at 317-572-3986,
or fax 317-572-4002.

Jossey-Bass also publishes its books in a variety of electronic formats. Some content that appears in
print may not be available in electronic books.

Library of Congress Cataloging-in-Publication Data

Davis, Ray, 1949-
      Leading for growth : how Umpqua Bank got cool and created a culture of greatness /
Ray Davis with Alan Shrader. — 1st ed.
          p. cm.
      "A Wiley Imprint."
      Includes bibliographical references and index.
      ISBN 978-0-7879-8607-0 (cloth)
      1. Organizational effectiveness. 2. Corporations—Growth. 3. Leadership. 4. Umpqua Bank.
I. Shrader, Alan, 1945- II. Title.
HD58.9.D39 2007
658.4'063—dc22   2006036604

Printed in the United States of America
FIRST EDITION
HB Printing   10 9 8 7 6 5 4 3 2 1

To Bobbi,
ilytmotu,
Ray

Contents

Introduction: There Is No Door Number Three   1

The pursuit of relentless growth has one underlying premise: You get better or you get worse. You can't stay the same. This book is for all companies that are tired of treading water.

PART ONE: PREREQUISITES FOR RELENTLESS GROWTH   7

1. **What Business Are You *Really* In?**   9

Umpqua started to take off when we decided we were really in the retail business, not just the banking business, and started learning from successful retailers like Nordstrom. This chapter offers advice to help you discover what business you are really in.

2. **Never-Ending Discipline**   23

Leaders need to realize that growth is not a project, not a quick fix. You must have the discipline to realize you never have it made.

3. **Have Positive Passion**   30

Be relentless about your vision. Know what you stand for. We call ourselves The World's Greatest Bank. It helps us stand out with our customers, but more than that, it creates positive passion within the company.

4. **Snap the Rubber Band Syndrome**   40

Each of us has a rubber band attached to our backside, connected to tradition. This chapter offers strategies to help people overcome the pull of comfortable routines.

5. **What's Going On Behind Your Back?**   49

Having the right strategy is meaningless unless you can execute it flawlessly on the ground. This chapter explains

how to put systems in place to inspect the execution of
strategy at the lowest level.

PART TWO: ROLES OF A LEADER   57

6.   **Support Your People—and Hold 'Em Accountable**   59

Leaders have many roles, but support and accountability
are critical—and they go hand in hand.

7.   **Give Them the Power**   69

In the past, the leader was the guy with the answers.
Today, you have to empower the people closest to the
action to come up with their own answers.

8.   **Rise Above the Battlefield**   79

Leaders need to rise above the battlefield to achieve a
strategic perspective on the company. I explain the tactics
I use to get above the fray and—just as important—how I
help the people on my executive team do this as well.

9.   **Explain Your Movie**   87

Leaders cannot delegate the job of explaining their vision
for the company—what I call "this movie that's playing in
my head."

10.   **Be Real**   94

If you can't be yourself, you can't lead. It's as simple
as that.

PART THREE: MASTER THE BASICS   101

11.   **Sweat the Small Stuff**   103

Every great company sweats the details. In this chapter,
I talk about how great companies such as Disney sweat
the small stuff.

12.   **Who Do You Want on Your Bus?**   109

In *Good to Great,* Jim Collins says that you've got to get the
right people on the bus. I think that is exactly right. But
who are the right people?

13.   **Keep Your Board Strong—and Informed**   118

Companies can't move fast if the executive team has to
drag the board of directors along with it. This chapter

describes how I work with my board to keep us all aligned and on track.

14. **Intangibles Matter Most** 128

In a service business like ours, the most important metrics measure things that are intangible.

PART FOUR: MARKETING, MARKETING, MARKETING 139

15. **Find the Revolution Before It Finds You** 141

Revolutions are going on all the time in consumer preferences, in technology, in marketing, and in other areas. We do a number of things at Umpqua to find these revolutions before they overwhelm us.

16. **Your Brand Is You** 150

People don't like faceless bureaucracies. They like real people, real personalities. We've achieved remarkable success by staying true to ourselves. Some people say we're corny, but it's who we are—and people respond.

17. **Serve the Customer** 158

This chapter details our Universal Associates program: every associate in our stores is trained to be able to handle any task a customer requires. This sharply sets us apart from our competition. What are you doing to set yourself apart?

18. **Put Design into Everything You Do** 165

Design encompasses much more than just the physical layout of stores or products. When design is used effectively, it brings every aspect of your business into alignment so that everything reinforces and supports everything else.

PART FIVE: LEADING YOUR CULTURE 173

19. **Be There** 175

Maintaining a culture is like raising a teenager. You're constantly checking in. "What are you doing? Where are you going? Who are you hanging out with?"

20. **Keep Your Balance** 184

Leading for growth is a high-wire act—and there are many dimensions to keeping your balance.

21. Remember Who You Are   193

The biggest danger of relentless growth is that your very growth will undermine the qualities that produced that growth in the first place. You've also got to know what not to change—what to maintain if you want to stay on track.

22. Mergers and Acquisitions Done Right   201

A lot of Umpqua's growth has come from acquisitions, which have the potential to disrupt or dilute the acquiring company's culture. We have not allowed that to happen.

Conclusion: Making Relentless Progress   211

The key to growth is making progress every single day.

Acknowledgments   215
The Authors   217
Index   219

LEADING FOR GROWTH

Introduction

There Is No Door Number Three

When I hear a business leader say, "We want to stay right where we are—we don't need to change," I'll sell my stock in that company right away. Companies can never stay the same. Leading for growth is not optional.

The simple fact is, you get better or you get worse. You cannot stay the same. There is no Door Number Three. Here's why. Suppose I row you out into a lake and tell you to jump in. I tell you to tread water. Then I tell you I'll be back in three days. When I come back, are you still treading water? No, either you swam back to shore, improving your situation, or you were stupid enough to drown. I guarantee you, you won't have stayed the same, treading water.

It's the same with business. Businesses that want to stay the same are trying to tread water indefinitely. And it doesn't work. Too many outside pressures and internal issues are going to create change, like it or not. I don't care if you're selling tires, insurance, consulting services, or furniture. Your company is going to change for better or worse. As a leader, you have to decide, "Are we going to get better (Door Number One) or get worse (Door Number Two)?"

Not much of a choice, is it?

Leading for growth isn't necessarily about getting bigger just to be bigger. It's about getting better, stronger, more agile, more customer focused, and becoming a relentless competitor. And companies that do that do get bigger—but it's a result, not an objective.

1

I'll admit, sometimes growing your business requires little more than a steady hand at the helm—companies in all sectors prospered in the boom years of the 1990s, for example. But what do you do when the tide isn't rising, when it may even be going out?

The boom years are long gone, yet a few companies continue to thrive, gaining market share day after day, month after month, year after year. Some of these companies are in brand-new growth industries, such as eBay and Google. But others are in industries that could hardly be classified as new or growing: retailing, manufacturing, and the like. Southwest Airlines is one such company. Another is the company I lead, which may be unknown to you if you don't live in the Pacific Northwest. It's called Umpqua Bank— and it has grown relentlessly over the past twelve years, going from $140 million in assets in 1994 to more than $7 billion today.

When I took the helm in 1994 as CEO of South Umpqua State Bank, as it was then known, it was a closely held company that employed sixty people in a rural, economically depressed region of Oregon. An hour and a half plane ride down the coast was Silicon Valley, just beginning the tremendous boom that would create millionaires by the score before petering out in the first year of the new century. They had computer chips and biotech and venture capitalists crawling all over the place. We had none of that. We had the timber industry and the Spotted Owl. Talk about a lack of synergy! And yet we grew our company.

Today Umpqua Holdings is a publicly traded company that employs eighteen hundred people throughout Oregon, Washington, and northern California—and has been featured in numerous financial industry publications as well as *Fast Company, BusinessWeek,* and on CNBC. The writers of these articles sometimes call us "quirky" or "cool"; almost all comment on our unique culture and how it has propelled our growth. They describe how one small company broke away from the pack of its more traditional rivals to create growing value for shareholders, customers, and employees.

Leading for Growth offers real-life lessons from my experiences in leading Umpqua on a journey of transformation that took it on a path of consistent growth year after year. This book is not intended to tell Umpqua's story. The strategies and methods I used had little to do with our particular financial services industry and everything to do with understanding how to motivate people, create a competitive advantage, ensure flawless execution, and meet the other challenges every business leader faces. I also bring in lessons that I have learned from companies I admire, such as Ritz-Carlton and Nordstrom for customer service and Nike and Apple Computer for marketing and design. This book offers practical, straightforward advice for all businesses on understanding the competitive landscape they face and on building and leading a great culture that generates relentless growth.

Do you have employees? Do you have customers? Do you want to lead the first group in ways that create more and more of the second? This book is for you.

What This Book Offers

With this book, I set out to offer a fresh look at how leaders can steer their companies to long-term success. Companies with consistent growth records understand their markets very well, execute their strategies precisely, consistently manage change, stay agile, and develop the discipline to maintain course.

This book will show you how to

- Discover what business you are really in and create your competitive advantage.
- Build an organization with committed and enthusiastic employees.
- Connect marketing strategy and execution on the ground.
- Create learning opportunities for all managers and staff.
- Fight "the rubber band syndrome" that often pulls people back into old routines.
- Rise above the day-to-day battlefield to achieve a strategic perspective on your company and where it is going.
- Stay agile by keeping the board informed and strategically aligned.
- Manage mergers and acquisitions in ways that support rather than dilute the culture.

Throughout, I emphasize what you can and should do personally in your leadership role. For example, I explain why you have to understand the real nature of change (it's not a process but a journey) and describe how you can protect yourself from conventional wisdom, which can endanger leadership (don't worry about being called unreasonable, for example).

This book will offer plain talk and useful advice based on Umpqua's actual experience. I have written it for all business leaders who want to grow their companies. I hope it will be especially attractive to those looking for something beyond the conventional wisdom—who are ready to look at leadership in a new way.

Overview of Contents

The first part of the book, "Prerequisites for Relentless Growth," explains the elements I believe you have to put in place before you can hope to grow your company. As a leader, it is your job to (1) cut through conventional wisdom and understand what business you are really in, (2) develop your own discipline and instill discipline in your company, (3) generate the positive passion that comes from a clear vision of your future, (4) create an atmosphere that propels people to embrace change, and (5) ensure that strategy and execution mesh on the ground. I devote a chapter to meeting each of these challenges.

Many factors go into taking a company on a path of sustained and relentless growth. It takes innovative product development, savvy marketing, strong execution, and much, much more. Many of these responsibilities can be delegated—but some cannot. Part Two, "Roles of a Leader," describes the essentials that a leader cannot delegate, the critical aspects of leading and managing that have to start at the top if they are to start anywhere. These critical roles include supporting your people, holding them accountable, empowering them, helping them gain perspective, and explaining the big picture to them. Moreover, all of these roles require you to be yourself as a leader.

There is no rocket science in Part Three, "Master the Basics," just commonsense nuts and bolts—but too often these basics get short shrift in books on leadership. You cannot transform your company if you aren't very good at getting the small stuff right. In this section of the book, I explain why you've got to sweat the small details—and offer advice on getting the right people on your bus,

it helps propel growth rather than
place to measure intangibles such

ks on leadership and none of them
ting. I don't think you can be very
mpany on a path of growth if you
to the market you serve. As HP
d to say, "Marketing is far too impor-
ng Department." In Part Four, "Mar-
," I look at the key roles of the leader
understands the realities of the mar-
often occur. I also talk about brand-
d the critical importance of design in
design is used effectively, it brings every
alignment so that everything reinforces
se.

≋ A Note on Motivational Moments ≋

One of the things that I talk about in this book is the importance of having fun at work. At Umpqua we start every day
with a motivational moment—a brief group activity (five minutes or less) that promotes fun and teamwork and often
teaches key lessons or provokes fresh ways to look at our business. Every department or team in the company is free to
choose what to do for its motivational moments. I have
included an actual motivational moment at the end of every
chapter that relates to the topic of the chapter. I hope you
find them *fun* and interesting and that they provoke new
ways for you to think about how you can lead for growth.

The final section of the book is perhaps the most important to
your long-term success in growing your company. The biggest danger of relentless growth is that growth itself can undermine the
qualities that made you grow in the first place. You can fight this
tendency by maintaining a strong culture. In Part Five, "Leading

Your Culture," I examine why culture is so important and explain how leaders can keep their culture on track, even as growth threatens to stretch core cultural values out of shape. Keeping your balance, holding on to your identity, and being very careful with mergers and acquisitions are critical to maintaining a strong culture. The Conclusion details critical leadership lessons on growth.

Come Along for the Ride

I hope the insights and lessons I offer will be useful to you as you take our experience and creatively apply it to help your business break away from the pack—and create a higher level of excitement for you as you explore new ways to lead for growth. Perhaps, like me, you will feel your heart beat just a little bit faster with anticipation at discovering an idea that can make a real difference in strengthening your business.

You can't grow your business without making it better, changing it in ways large and small. If you want a book that tells you how to keep your business healthy while leaving it unchanged, this isn't the book for you. If you want a book that offers guidance on doing what it takes to grow your business day after day, year after year, and have fun doing it, then I hope you'll come along for the ride. Remember, there is no Door Number Three.

Part One

Prerequisites for Relentless Growth

Many ingredients are needed to take a company on a path of sustained and relentless growth. It takes talented people, strong marketing, precise execution, the right metrics, and much, much more. I'll give you my take on these growth ingredients later on in this book. My view is that all these factors don't matter a whole lot without strong, effective leadership. So that's what I am going to focus on first.

Leading for Growth Starts with You

If you are leading a company large or small, or a profit center in a larger company, you need to realize that it all starts with you. It doesn't all depend on you. (Only an egomaniac would think the company's success all depends on him or her.) But make no mistake, as a leader, it all starts with you. That's why I call this section of the book *prerequisites* for relentless growth.

   If you don't have what it takes, if you don't focus on the right things in the right way, then I don't care what great business plan you have or how big your line of credit is, you are probably going to stumble somewhere along the way.

What are the leadership prerequisites that you need to master? I think they boil down to five key essentials:

- You have to cut through conventional wisdom and figure out what business you are really in.
- You must develop the self-discipline to stay true to your plan in the face of conventional wisdom and other obstacles.
- You need to generate the positive passion that comes from a clear vision of your future.
- You must make it clear to your people that you are personally involved in leading them through the changes ahead.
- You have to develop the ability to find out what's going on behind your back to ensure your strategies' being implemented effectively on the ground.

These five key responsibilities belong to you as a leader. They cannot be delegated. That is why I say it all starts with you.

Chapter 1

What Business Are You *Really* In?

Industry publications write about Umpqua a lot. And they usually say nice things, remarking on our strong growth, our return to shareholders, our reputation for being cool and quirky, and our unique organizational culture. But these articles almost always insert a comment that irks me. No matter how positive the article is, it almost always says something like, "Umpqua Bank calls its branches 'stores,'" as if the word *store* is a gimmick. They humor us by putting *store* in quotation marks, as if real grown-up bankers wouldn't be so silly as to call their branches that. But it's not a gimmick. It's part of who we are and how we see our business. They don't understand that it's a huge, even dinosaur-sized, part of the reason they are writing about us in the first place! It's part of our unique culture that they extol.

Why do we call our facilities *stores* rather than *branches?* Because we understand what business we are really in. We're in the retail service business, which to us means we sell banking products and services to the public in our stores. In this chapter, I explain exactly what I mean by that and why it is so important for you to understand what business you are really in.

Business Not as Usual

It is too easy to look at your company and say, "we're in the banking business." (Or in the tire business or the computer business.) You will never break free of the hold of conventional wisdom with that kind of thinking. And if you can't break free of conventional wisdom, you'll never break out of the pack—you'll never create a competitive edge that separates you from your competitors.

To illustrate how a lack of understanding of what business you are really in can do to you, just consider Steve Jobs and Apple Computer.

Back in the early 1980s Jobs thought that his company was in the computer business, specifically the computer hardware business, and that it could prosper by selling better computers than its competitors. And for a while, that worked. Then IBM entered the picture, along with its then-partner Microsoft. In 1984, Apple tried to jump ahead by introducing the first point-and-click operating system with its revolutionary new line of Macintosh computers—a great leap forward that was much easier to use than Microsoft's cumbersome DOS system. But unfortunately, Jobs never realized that the business was changing and that he was now competing in the software business. He and his successor John Sculley kept the Mac operating system proprietary and used it only as a way to sell Apple's hardware.

Apple thought it was competing against IBM, Compaq, and the other PC clones when it was really competing against Microsoft. When Microsoft copied the look and feel of the Macintosh system with Windows—and sold it to every comer—Apple's goose was cooked. Of course, Apple faced many hurdles—who knows what might have happened if Jobs hadn't been forced from the company? But it's my firm opinion that if Jobs had understood early on that he was really in the software business, we probably wouldn't know Bill Gates as the world's richest man.

So understanding what business you are really in is absolutely critical to success.

"Okay," you might say, "that's an extreme example from the early days of a revolutionary new industry that was growing exponentially and whose landscape was changing daily. I'm in a mature industry that's growing slowly, even in good years. How does that apply to me?"

Well, it applies to you in spades! And Umpqua is living proof. After all, banking is a mature business if there ever was one—banks have been around for hundreds of years! Walk around any city, any small town, and you'll see a dozen banks in a few blocks. And don't talk to me about growth! When we started to reinvent Umpqua Bank in 1994, our market was in the midst of profound economic slump. The economy in our region was rooted in the timber industry—and just happened to be the home of the Spotted Owl and a strong environmental movement. Talk about total lack of synergy. The economy was at a standstill, our market wasn't growing, and yet we found a way to make Umpqua grow, moving from third in market share to first in just three years in our home market. How did we do it? For starters, we had to kill conventional wisdom in the company. We had to stop our people from thinking like bankers and get them to think like people in the business we were really in: retail service.

Most businesses are run on conventional wisdom, and they struggle to get by. Every quarter it's the same story. Are we meeting our numbers? Are sales up? You cannot grow your business by feeding it conventional wisdom. And you cannot grow your business if all you are doing is worrying about your numbers—because then you are not honing a strategy to seize the future. As the new leader at Umpqua, my first job priority in reinventing the company was to kill the conventional wisdom that had guided the company for forty years. The bank's board had hired me to take this small company and make it grow. Together we decided to seize the future.

> You cannot grow your business if all you are doing is worrying about your numbers.

But let me go back to the beginning.

Seizing the Future

When I was contacted about running Umpqua in 1994, it was a small community bank in rural Oregon with $140 million in assets and six small branches. It was called South Umpqua State Bank, even though there wasn't a North Umpqua State Bank. The previous CEO had retired, and the board was looking for a change. The bank was at a crossroads. It was a solid bank and well respected in the small communities it served. But it wasn't really going anywhere, and by continuing to practice the purest definition of insanity (doing the same thing over and over again while expecting different results) the company was doomed to go nowhere and in fact its future would have been doubtful. The big banks smelled blood and were sniffing around, looking for prey—in our world, acquisitions.

When the board interviewed me for the CEO position, I told them that if they wanted things to stay the same, I wasn't their man. But if they wanted to employ a strategy that might have a good chance of creating shareholder value, then I might be a candidate. Fortunately for me the board realized that if they were serious about creating value for the shareholders and improving the overall intrinsic value of the company, they would have to support dramatic changes in how it operated, marketed, hired people, and the like. In fact we had to reinvent the entire institution, and build it around the principles and practices of the business we were really in. The board bit the bullet and took a chance with me—an unproven character from Atlanta, Georgia.

Before coming to Umpqua I had run a bank management consulting firm and dealt with CEOs from all sizes of banks across the United States. I learned a lot in dealing with all these different bankers. In fact, it was like attending graduate school. I learned what *not* to do, from helping people fix some of the stupidest mistakes they could have made. I also picked up some pretty good ideas. But overall, I was amazed by the lack of creativity at the top levels and felt that I could take my ten years of consulting experience and put it to work in a small bank with a well-defined market and hopefully create something interesting.

Here's why.

What had struck me during my years of consulting and traveling around the country, going to all these different banks, was how similar they all were—and how bland. You know from your own experience that the typical bank is quiet, cold, and boring. It has ropes to keep people in line, empty desks, and stale coffee. You can see how bored the people in line are. Often the tellers aren't much more animated. Sure, you'll get a shy smile and a weak "thank you," but two minutes after you walk out, you'll have forgotten the whole experience. I could put you down in almost any bank in the country, and you'd know right away you were in a bank, but ninety-nine times out of a hundred you'd have no idea *what* bank. They are *all* the same. I started to think that if you created a bank environment that was distinctive, attractive, and inviting, with great customer service, you might be able to give your bank an identity that people would respond to.

> Think of your own business and industry. What do you and your competitors do that is boring, stale, or bland?

Think of your own business and industry. What do you and your competitors do that is boring, stale, or bland? Is there something that is numbingly similar across every company, including yours? If so, you have a great opportunity.

I also realized that we would not be successful in differentiating Umpqua with resources, people, computers, locations, saturation-marketing campaigns, you name it. We were a tiny outfit; the big guys had bigger guns—they had already won that battle. And I knew full well that bank products are for the most part commodities. Sure, different banks will have slightly different loan terms, savings rates, and check colors, but they are all similar. So I felt there was little to no opportunity to have Umpqua stand out with products. Even if we were capable of creating a new and exciting product, I knew it would be copied by a competitor down the street within a few days.

I got together with my management team and we started asking ourselves questions: Why would somebody want to bank with us? Here we were in a depressed market, competing against all the big national players as well as credit unions and other community banks. How were we going to stand out? How were we going to get people to drive by two or three of our competitors' branches to bank with Umpqua? We realized that we had no answers to these questions as things currently stood. If we wanted to grow, we had to *create* answers to these questions.

If you sell tires, it's the same question, why would somebody want to buy tires from you? Why wouldn't they just go to the nearest tire store? Why would someone be inconvenienced and drive past two stores to get to your store? These questions were critical to our survival.

Think about your business. How do you stand out? Why should someone do business with you over another competitor with virtually the same products and services? How are you differentiating your department, division, or company so you stand out from the pack? How you answer these questions is critical to *your* survival.

I frequently tell people that the radical changes that we were going through began with a motion picture that played only in my head. It was always very specific in that it had a beginning and ultimately a happy ending that showed where we wanted to go—but the middle, which showed how we were going to get there, was always changing as the movie played out in my imagination. It depicted (to me at least) what it would be like to walk into a bank that people *did* want to hang out in, that was exciting, that was, just maybe, even a little bit cool. The movie that was playing in my mind was fuzzy around the edges at first, but one thing I saw clearly was the potential to significantly differentiate our company from our competitors and allow our customers and clients who entered an Umpqua store to know right away what bank they were in—Umpqua! Through this crazy little movie I had already started to think of Umpqua as not just another bank, but as something else entirely.

I kept playing that movie in my mind, over and over, people walking into a bank that was exciting and made them want to linger a while. Where do people hang out? Starbucks, of course. Lots of people also like to go to the mall and hang out at Nordstrom or the Gap. But those were very different businesses. Or were they? And that's when I started to focus on the larger picture of understanding exactly what industry we *really* competed in. Of course I realized that since Umpqua is a bank we clearly competed within the financial industry. However, I also realized that banks also compete in the retail service industry. Think about it, financial institutions sell products and services just like the companies that sell perfume, Levi's, or coffee. Retailers have stores. So do banks, only they call them branches . . . for some reason.

What would Umpqua look like if we recreated it from the ground up as a retailer that just happens to sell financial services? Retailers work hard to make their stores attractive, even exciting, and focus on displaying the products and services they sell. They know how to draw customers into their stores and motivate those customers to buy. The best of them know how to build outstanding customer loyalty.

The movie in my head started to become more vivid. What if, like Nordstrom, we created an environment that drew our customers back into the store frequently to browse through our products, making it easy for them to interact with and ultimately purchase our services? After all, market research shows that two-thirds of consumer purchases are impulse buys.

I started talking about this movie (yep, still playing in my head)—my vision for Umpqua bank—to my management team. I told them, "Nobody goes to hang out at the local bank, just to kill a few hours, as people do at Nordstrom or Starbucks." I asked them to imagine what Umpqua would look like if we decided to see ourselves as a retailer offering financial services. How would our stores (not branches) look? How would we do things differently? Could we actually entice people to come in just to hang out? How would we operate? How would we train our people?

Reinventing Our Business

We didn't have all the answers at first, of course, but slowly things started to change.

One of the first things we did was to stop hiring people who had a banking background and nothing else. Since we wanted to transform ourselves into a retailer, we looked for people with a retail background. (As I said, *This ain't rocket science, folks!*) For a teller position we would hire someone who perhaps worked at the Gap since their job was to dazzle people who came to the store, know their product line, help customers find what they were looking for, suggest other things to buy, and make sales. These people were used to working on their feet and understood the sales process. Compare a person with a retail sales background to a person who had been a teller for ten years—sitting behind a teller window and never selling a thing from one year to the next. Who would you hire? Most bankers would have hired the teller, of course. Not us.

I also sent teams of people on road trips to different cities and asked them to look at companies that have a reputation for some sort of pizzazz, places like Restoration Hardware, the Gap, Nordstrom, even a luxury hotel. I told them, "I want you to observe.

Use all your senses, find out what things look, feel, smell like. And when you come back, I want you to step out of the day-to-day, forget about how banks are supposed to operate, and use your imagination to think about how this might apply to us."

As we went along, we made a lot of small changes, which I won't bore you with here. Then, in early 1996, we thought we were ready to assemble everything we'd learned into what we called our first concept store. We built this new store in Roseburg, Oregon, near our headquarters at the time. It was a $4 million project for us, a serious investment for a company our size. We hired a consultant to help us plan the design—and it wasn't one of the bank consultants, because we knew what they would offer. Since we had decided we were really in the retail business, we hired a consultant who focused on retail design and marketing—Charlene Stern of Stern Marketing, a true professional. She challenged us to break free of ideas that might still be holding us back and to really focus on the retail experience we were trying to create. (And I must say, her advice was superb; we received an incredibly positive response from our customers when we opened the store.)

But a building does not make a store. To make the store work, it would take people. Good people. Creative people. I made a deal with my executive vice president of retail, Steve May, that allowed me to personally hire the people to staff the concept store. I was not looking for job skills. I was looking for energy, a twinkle in the eye that says, *I can do it; I am capable of anything, if you give me the tools.* That last part is critical. I found great people, but I had to give them the tools. That was my responsibility.

So before the new store opened, we rented a suite at a local hotel and conducted an intense six-week training program for the store's newly formed team. We made sure they had a full understanding of all our products and services, so each one could help any of our customers with anything they needed. We also focused on sales techniques, manners, and other retail service skills.

Finally, the builders were done with all the finishing work and our people were ready and eager to open the doors to the new store—shown in Figure 1.1. And it made quite an impression. It certainly looked like the sort of place where people would want to hang out. We had a computer café with free Internet access and our very own Umpqua brand coffee, an "Investment Opportunity

FIGURE 1.1   UMPQUA'S ROSEBURG STORE

Center" for investment type products, and a "Serious About Service Center," that offered general information and had a phone that connected right to my direct line. Anybody with a problem was invited to call the CEO.

This was so different from a bank that at first we had a number of customers who would step in for the first time, look around, and go right back out to look at the sign over the door, to make sure they were in the right place.

They'd come back in, a grin on their faces, and ask, "Is this really Umpqua Bank?" When one of the associates assured them that it was, the response was often, "Wow."

That was just the reaction I was hoping for. And before long, people actually started to hang out at Umpqua Bank!

Our competitors in town thought we were nuts. But not for long, not when their customers started to become our customers.

You see, our first concept store, embodying our commitment to the retail business we were really in, created a significant competitive advantage over our competitors. And it quickly moved Umpqua up to be one of the fastest-growing community banks in the Northwest. Within three years of the introduction of our new retail strategy in this market we had become number 1 in market share and today we control over 43 percent of this market. (Figure 1.2 shows ads illustrating our retail concept.)

As word of our success spread over the next ten years, banks from all over the world, including small community banks and giants such as Citigroup and London's HSBC, came to see how Umpqua has successfully differentiated itself. They are usually drawn to us by an article or photo of our new store design that appeared in one of those magazines that refuse to refer to our stores without quotation marks. These bankers come to learn our secrets: our non–rocket-scientist formulas that when you get right down to it are really just basic sound management and marketing strategies that work!

When they visit, they kick the tires, take pictures of our stores, sip our coffee, and make notes on our design and floor plans.

FIGURE 1.2   UMPQUA ADS

However, after they see how our stores look and feel, it doesn't take long for them to zero in on the things that have really made us stand out. Even though they have come to us to visit our store design and product delivery system, what they really want to know is the answer to this question, which is asked on every visit: "How do you get your people to act the way they do with your customers?"

You see, for us, understanding what business we are really in is not just a gimmick; nor is it just a matter of hiring an architect to build a fancy store—any company can do that. Seeing ourselves as a retailer extends far beyond selling coffee mugs and T-shirts. It affects how we hire, train, and reward our staff; how we measure ourselves; and—most important—how we shape our corporate culture and the values it embodies. Our culture is unique, and I describe it at length in Part Five. It's why we feel secure in giving these tours to our potential competitors. They can copy the look of our stores, but they can't copy our culture, our DNA.

What Business Are *You* Really In?

Understanding what business you are really in is not so much a discovery as a willful act of creation. When everyone in your industry is playing by one set of rules, you must decide to play by another. We decided to play by retail rules rather than banking rules. This is especially important if you compete in an industry that basically offers products or services that are commodities. The only way to break away from the pack in such a situation is to start operating on a different playing field.

> When everyone in your industry is playing by one set of rules, you must decide to play by another.

When you move to reorient your company around the business you are really in, you'll find it will lead to changes in almost everything you do. You'll need to rethink many of the key dimensions of your business:

- What success looks like
- How performance is measured
- Marketing objectives and strategies
- Hiring and other personnel issues
- Rewards and incentives
- Culture issues
- Customer relations

I'll discuss all these issues in later chapters.

Too many businesses look only at their competitors. Benchmarking your company's performance against your peers or competitors was a big fad awhile back. The idea was that you'd identify who was best in your industry at doing something, and then try to match their approach and standards. Now, all that will do is make you as good as (the same as) your competitors. Decide if you just want to tread water (which you can't do forever) or want to grow your company and stand out. Ask yourself what you are doing to get people to switch from your competitor to you. To make your business stand out, you will need to think about your business differently from the way your competitors do.

How can you uncover what business you want to be in? Here are a few ideas to get you started:

Find a business you admire that is outside your industry and study it. Nordstrom was not Umpqua's competitor, but it was similar to us in that it was in the retail business, as we were, although it sold clothes and we sold financial services. We set out to learn from Nordstrom and other retailers that provided excellent customer service, not from Citibank. Study and visit businesses that are not competitors but are similar to your business in some way. What can you learn from them? How can you twist what they do and apply it to your business? I promise you, your competitors are not doing this. Just taking this small step will give you an advantage over others.

Look for the conventional wisdom in your business or industry. The more sacred the cow is, the better. Challenge it. How would things change if you stopped doing X or Y or did them differently? Killing conventional wisdom is only the first step, but it is an essential step.

Get off the battlefield and take a bird's-eye view. Whatever business you are in, you are also in a larger category. We knew we were in the banking business, but what truly expanded our minds was when we realized we were also in the retail service business, just like Nordstrom. If you sell tires, you're also in the automotive business. If you're a travel agent, you're in the entertainment industry. Or do you primarily serve business customers? Then see yourself as providing business services. How would that change the way you do business?

Recreate your business with a blank piece of paper. Imagine that your business was wiped out by a hurricane or earthquake and you received its full value from your insurance. How would you rebuild it?

Legendary management guru Peter Drucker pointed out that every organization operates on a *Theory of the Business,* that is, a set of assumptions as to what its business is, what its objectives are, how it defines results, who its customers are, what the customers value and pay for. Much of the time, this theory is unarticulated and doesn't go an inch beyond the conventional wisdom of the industry a company operates in. When you start to examine what business you are *really* in, you'll uncover the assumptions that you have been using, and then you'll have an opportunity to change them.

A Final Word

Here's a word of caution: saying that we are in the retail business doesn't mean we don't have to be very, very good as a bank. It means that we have to be very good as a bank *and* as a retailer. We have to live up to high banking standards *and* high retail service standards. That makes all of our jobs just a little harder.

But we don't mind.

We take pride in our company. Ask any of our associates and they'll tell you, "You've got to be *good* to work at Umpqua!"

MOTIVATIONAL MOMENT

Thinking "Outside the Boxes"

Exercise: In the following line of letters, cross out six letters so that the remaining letters, without altering their sequence, will spell a familiar English word.

BSAINXLEATNTEARS

Answer: Cross off "SIXLETTERS" and the remaining word is BANANA. This exercise encourages associates to look at things differently—most associates will be searching and selecting six different letters to cross off. The exercise shows them to keep an open mind and remember there is always another way to look at things.

There is always another way to look at what business you are in. Think about it!
    —Ray

Chapter 2

Never-Ending Discipline

Here's a true story. I've stayed at Ritz-Carlton hotels for many years. If you've ever been to one of their hotels, you know how exemplary their service is. The company motto is, "We are ladies and gentlemen serving ladies and gentlemen." Ritz-Carlton is the only hotel company to win the Malcolm Baldrige National Quality Award and the only service company to receive this prestigious award twice. They also have their own internal service awards. One time on a business trip to Atlanta, I checked into the Ritz-Carlton in Buckhead. I knew about their internal quality awards, and I got talking to the bellman who was taking me up to my room. (I like talking to the frontline workers. They'll be honest with you.) As we were going up in the elevator, I asked the bellman, "How'd you do in the quality program?"

He seemed a little surprised. "Oh, Mr. Davis, you know about that?"

"Yes, so how did you do last month?"

"Well, Mr. Davis, we failed."

"What?" I blurted. "You always ranked up near the top! What happened?"

"Housekeeping."

"Housekeeping? What did they do?"

"It was the *TV Guides*."

I didn't understand what he was getting at. "Did they forget to put new *TV Guides* in each room for the week?"

"No, sir. They forgot to move the bookmark ribbons every day."

I was astounded. *That* is attention to detail. Some people may think this example of attention to detail is extreme, that it is taking service discipline way over the top. Not me. When I heard what the bellman said, I was immediately impressed by the incredible focus and discipline required to achieve the standard of service they set. Think about it: if you're another hotel chain and you don't have that discipline, how do you compete against these guys? And of course, with that level of discipline, they can charge more for their rooms and people are happy to pay.

Look in the Mirror

When you are serious about leading for growth, discipline is the never-ending story. Discipline always starts at the top—with you, the leader. Discipline has always been and will always be the most challenging aspect of a leader's job. I'm not talking about the type of discipline where you punish others for wrong behavior; I'm talking about *self-discipline,* the mental tenacity required of leaders to plant their strategy and stick with it day in and day out, through good times and bad. Enforcing standards is important, of course, but you can have all the rules in the world and it won't matter one bit if you yourself don't have the perseverance to stay true to your vision, your plans for growth. You've got to look in the mirror first.

Discipline is hard because if you really set yourself a new course, a challenging path, you'll soon find all sorts of people telling you to "be reasonable." You'll find conventional wisdom coming at you from a dozen directions telling you that what you're trying to do is impossible, or too hard, or not really important, and besides, it won't work anyway. "Be reasonable," you'll hear, "you can't really expect us to do that"—whatever *that* is.

> Discipline always starts at the top—with the leader.

I'm sure a manager at Ritz-Carlton said at some point, "We can't follow housekeepers around to make sure they move the bookmarks in the *TV Guides*. Be reasonable." Spending time and effort (which equal money) on something so trivial as bookmarks in *TV Guides* does seem unreasonable. But what is even more unreasonable—and foolish—is deciding on a key competitive strategy and then not following through to make sure that strategy is being implemented as well as humanly possible.

As a leader, you have to be tough enough to appear unyielding and unreasonable. *These are our standards. This is what we are going to do. This is what we are going to become, and heaven help anyone who tries to bring conventional wisdom in here to stop us.* Discipline is about your vision, about that movie that plays in your head that shows where your company is going and what it is going to become. If you've figured out what business you are really in, what makes you different from all the other companies out there, you have a vision of what you're going to become. If you're smart, you realize you're not going to get there in a straight line. You'll have ups and downs, starts and stops. Discipline means you are never going to give up. An old proverb defines success this way: Fall down six times, get up seven. And that's what discipline means: you keep going.

Naturally, all strategies evolve over time and need fine-tuning. But your vision for the company is about more than strategy, and it should not change dramatically unless you have completely lost confidence in the direction you're headed. Certainly, market shifts, competitor moves, world events, and other external conditions no leader has any control over can affect the feasibility of your vision. When these occur you must be able to ascertain the effect these surprises have on the company's ability to achieve the vision and adjust accordingly. But unless something occurs that renders the vision impotent, you need to have the discipline to keep going.

The point is *there is always a test going on,* a test of the leader's resolve in implementing the strategy. These tests come in all sorts of guises—and sometimes don't even seem like challenges to your vision. And if you're not careful, you'll go off course and not even realize it. For example, we developed a new deposit product at Umpqua a few years ago. We had high hopes for it and had planned a significant marketing campaign around it. After a lot of planning, coordination with marketing, and training our staff in selling the new product, I got a real shocker in our final launch meeting before rolling it out. The technology team reported that due to a change in our newly "upgraded" system, it would not be able to support the new product after all. They went on at length with technical details about the limitations of our software, but the upshot was, they said, that our new product could not be offered. Now I'm not very savvy when it comes to technology and I had no way of judging the technical explanation they offered. But I knew all the execs around the table were looking at me, wondering about my reaction. I let the silence build as they waited for my response.

> There is always a test going on, a test of the leader's resolve.

Finally, after thinking things over a bit, I said softly that it was really too bad they couldn't support the new product, because we were launching it as planned. And I asked the tech team to make arrangements to keep track of the product manually until the software could be fixed. They left that meeting in shock! I'm sure they thought I was being completely unreasonable. But I don't think so: I sent a message to all involved that I was deadly serious about making progress and would not be talked out of it over technology shortfalls or anything else. The issue wasn't technology—it was whether we had the discipline to stay the course. They got the message! What was really interesting was that within two days of launch the tech team called me with "Great news!" They had figured out how to adjust the software in time. I wasn't surprised.

Any time you have people around you asking you in so many words to be reasonable, put your guard up. This does not mean you should not listen. It means you need to listen to those ideas that will help your plan succeed, help it evolve, recolor it, rename it—but stay the course.

Spread Discipline Throughout the Organization

People below and people above you on the food chain will test you and your commitment daily. What you say and how you say it will always be evaluated for weakness or change of mind. For example, if you are the CEO of your company and work with a board of directors, how committed are the directors to what you are trying to accomplish? It must become their strategy as much as yours. Do they have the guts to stay with you as you build your company? And I mean through the tough times when it appears you aren't making progress as fast as you want. (I'll talk about dealing with your board in Chapter Thirteen.)

The most important set of eyes watching you belong to the people below you. Should they sense any hesitation through your comments or actions they will not follow you, period.

I tell my execs this all the time. When you are a leader, your people watch every move you make, and they want to know, are you committed or not? And if you act like something is not a big deal, let's not worry about it, then they are not going to worry about it. And that's why you've got to be relentless, unyielding, and even unreasonable. If you ever let up, then people are going to sense that maybe it isn't that big a deal and let up as well. If that happens, you've got to recreate the momentum. Had I acted as if dropping the ball on the new product launch was no big deal, I would have told everyone that our plans for the company weren't all that important. What a terrible message that would have been.

Discipline starts at the top, as I said earlier. But it has to spread to every part of the organization. Once you've got your own discipline to stay the course established, then you've got to ensure that everyone else—from the C-suite to the front lines—is also committed to taking the company where it has to go. Most of your people do not need a translator for the messages you deliver. Tell them yourself. I don't care how small or how big your company is, find ways to do this. As Nike says, just do it!

Many CEOs think that they are the only ones with their oars in the water, and that's why the boat is moving. Of course, sometimes that's true. But if you have one company where the CEO is the only one rowing, and another company where the CEO has the vast majority of the people rowing too—because they understand where they're going, they understand the commitment that's required to make it happen, and they understand what that means to them—you know which boat is going to pull ahead. Discipline is what makes it possible for us all to work together to achieve our goals.

The D-Word

There is no reason for people to be fearful of the *d-word,* as I call it. *Discipline* is not a bad word. Discipline describes what we have got to have if we are going to achieve our goals. Discipline doesn't always mean doing things exactly one way; there's some wiggle room. But the discipline button is always on, not off.

When discipline is handled correctly, it creates a powerful and positive environment. Here's another true story. As I mentioned, we made a lot of changes when I joined Umpqua. We started new programs and started measuring things so we could hold people accountable. I was talking about accountability and discipline every chance I got. Talk, talk, talk. Then I got e-mail from one of our associates really far down in the chain of command who worked in one of our stores. She said, "Ray, you've told us to make these changes and measure these things, but you haven't come around to tell us how we are doing. Why won't you hold us accountable?"

> The discipline button is always on, not off.

I felt like a big pitcher of ice cold water had been thrown in my face. I'd been out there flapping my lips about accountability, and here was someone saying, "Bring it on, big guy." This was a woman who said, "Okay, I get it. I think I know what you want me to do. I'm going to go to work. And I want some recognition." Suppose she had achieved a major portion of her goals and no one came around and said, "Hey, way to go!" Then she and everyone she talked to would wonder, Do these big shots believe in what they say or not? Because if they're not going to come back and say great job or hey you've got to do better, why are we doing this? Why are they having these meetings and talking so much when it's not that big a deal to them?

I didn't hold them accountable enough at the beginning. I was giving them way too much leeway to get moving ahead on reshaping our company, when they were basically saying, "Let's go, we're ready. We're not scared of that. We're going to do well. Don't make *us* push *you.*" Little victories like that win major battles. If I hadn't gone the next step to really hold people accountable, they would have become very disillusioned. That's why I say discipline creates a positive environment for everyone. It's discipline that aligns words and actions.

Another reason you have to be unyielding is that so many people are cynical about what they see as the latest fad of the month. They've been conditioned by bad management to expect that new programs introduced with bold announcements will eventually peter out. When I started reshaping Umpqua, that's what everyone thought. Two years later, they told me, "Ray, in that first meeting, we saw you come in as the new CEO with big ideas, and we just knew if we waited six weeks, your big plans would go away. But Ray, the difference with you was, they just never went away." Without the discipline to stay the course, we would have imploded. We would not have grown as fast as we have; we would not now be doing the things we're doing now.

Staying the course is all about being disciplined. In the matter of style and managing people, I'm not the most consistent. But when it comes to where we are going and how we are going to get there, I'm the most consistent guy in the world.

 MOTIVATIONAL MOMENT
Simon Says

Exercise: Play a simple game of Simon Says. Keep things moving quickly. If everyone does what "Simon" says to do and stays in the game, comment on how the "power of discipline" in customer service is essential to success. If you have numerous participants who goof up the instructions and have to sit down, comment on how important it is for each of us to stay focused, and that we want everyone to remain standing.

Chapter 3

Have Positive Passion

In Chapter Two, I talked about how discipline can create a positive environment for the people in your organization. But discipline without positive passion is like a car without gasoline. You may have a Rolls Royce or a Maserati—precision machines crafted with tremendous discipline—but without gas, you aren't going anywhere.

Positive passion is the fuel you need to propel your company to greatness.

Passion is boundless enthusiasm for your vision. *Positive* passion is that kind of enthusiasm coupled with optimism. Not only are you passionate about your vision, you believe you can and will achieve it. "Optimism doesn't wait on facts," author Norman Cousins wrote. "It deals in prospects."

Rudy Giuliani, who knows something about leadership and wrote a best-selling book about it, says that optimism is one of six key leadership principles. I recently had an opportunity to hear Giuliani speak on leadership. Here is why he thinks optimism is so important:

> People believe in leaders who have strong convictions and confidence. The optimism of a leader directly contributes to an organization's ability to succeed. Optimism, coupled with steadfast resolve, conveys a culture of confidence and helps organizations move successfully toward a common goal.

Who would follow someone who doesn't believe—with passion—that the goal is attainable? Can any leader succeed unless people throughout the organization passionately believe in the goal and that it is reachable? The questions answer themselves.

Discipline without passion leads to rigid adherence to rules, bureaucracy of the worst sort. Adding passion and optimism to discipline provides the impetus for constantly challenging and renewing the rules because you are on a quest to achieve something great. You need both: discipline *and* positive passion.

If you want to lead your company to new heights, you must be relentlessly passionate about your vision, *even if you are perceived as being unreasonable.* Know what you stand for. At Umpqua, we do. We call ourselves "The World's Greatest Bank." It might sound corny; it might even sound *unreasonable* for a regional bank in the Pacific Northwest. But we really believe it—and we're passionate about it!

> We call ourselves "The World's Greatest Bank." It might sound corny, but we really believe it—and we're passionate about it!

Vision Ignites Passion

Vision is important for leaders, because vision is what ignites passion. Let me tell you about how Umpqua's current vision came about. It's an interesting story.

As I discussed in Chapter One, when I came to what was then South Umpqua State Bank in 1994, I had this movie running in my head about the sort of bank I wanted to create, a place like Starbucks or Nordstrom where people would want to hang out. We decided that the business we were really in was the retail services industry, and that we would shape our training, our culture, our reward systems—in fact everything—around the concept of delivering an excellent retail experience to our customers. At the time I thought that if we looked like a Nordstrom and delivered excellent service, we had a chance for success. We didn't have a more specific vision than that. But it was enough to get us excited about moving in a new direction. And it guided the design of our first concept store in Roseburg, also described in Chapter One.

Because I was so passionate about recasting Umpqua in the mold of a retail store, I really tried to inspire others to make it their own—to take it and run with it. And they did—in a way that completely surprised me.

Shortly after we opened our bold new concept store in Roseburg, I bought the book *Raving Fans* (by Ken Blanchard and Sheldon Bowles) for all the staff at Umpqua. It was a fun book and we had a good time talking about it.

In the book, Blanchard and Sheldon tell the story of a gas station owner. Every time someone would pull into his station, the service attendant would say, "Welcome to the world's greatest service station." Over and over again. "Welcome to the world's greatest service station." Eventually, according to the book, everybody in town started calling it the World's Greatest Service Station.

We talked a lot about that at headquarters with Neal Brown, who was the manager of our new Roseburg concept store, and with other store managers. We talked about wanting to position ourselves as the world's greatest bank, but we didn't go any further than that. Then I went away on vacation. When I came back from vacation I drove by the Roseburg store, which was on the way to my house. I have to admit I was surprised when I saw a banner on the store, maybe five feet high and fifty feet long, stretching the length of the building. It said, "Welcome to the World's Greatest Bank." Neal, the store manager I had personally selected for this important post, hadn't said a word to me about doing this, much less gotten permission. I stopped the car and thought about going in and asking Neal what was going on, but it had been a long day and my family was tired, so I kept going. But the next morning I called the store as soon as I got to the office.

"Umpqua Bank," an associate answered, "how can I help you?"

I asked to speak to Neal. He got on the line, all excited: "Hey, what do you think? What do you think?"

I responded, "What do you mean?" playing dumb.

"Didn't you see our banner? The World's Greatest Bank! What do you think?"

"I did see the banner, Neal. I think it's pretty cool. But I have one question for you. If you are the world's greatest bank, why are you answering the phone just like any other bank? If you're not going to be proactive about being the world's greatest bank, you should take that banner down." I said I'd see him later and hung up.

Later that afternoon, I had to call back on something, and they answered the phone, "Welcome to The World's Greatest Bank. How can I help you?" And that's how it got started. Neal, a great guy, is still with the bank, by the way.

When Neal put up that banner, it was a surprise to everybody. Neal took it upon himself to say, *Let's go for it.* Neal was empowered to run his store. He took a chance, he really stuck out his chin. He put that banner up and waited to find out what would happen. The Roseburg store was our first concept store. It was nothing like any bank had ever tried. It had the computer café, the slide show for people waiting in line. The fact that it really was unique probably made it easier for Neal to put that sign up.

When Neal put up that banner, he was making a commitment. And that's what I reminded him of when I called to say he had to be proactive about being the world's greatest bank or take the banner down. But the thing about passion is that it inspires people to think like that *in the first place,* to take those chances. Lots of people are 8-to-5, clock in, clock out. They're not thinking about how to make the company better. My passion for transforming Umpqua turned out to be contagious. And it infected Neal. He was probably thinking, "I bet we can blow this place away if we put up the sign and live up to it." Well, I'll let Neal tell you in his own words what he was thinking:

> I thought I could get away with putting up the banner because we were always encouraged to have an entrepreneurial spirit and Ray instilled in us that it's okay to make mistakes if we own up to them, learn from them, move on, and do it differently next time.
>
> Having read *Raving Fans,* I just thought "The World's Greatest Bank" was an appropriate expectation to set for our customers, one that we would have to live up to. The point wasn't that we were already the world's greatest bank, but it was something we aspired to do and be.
>
> More than anything, it set an expectation for our people that we had to live up to. And even if we made a mistake, it put an expectation there that we had to make it right. Suppose a customer calls

up and an associate answers with "Welcome to the World's Greatest Bank." When the customer explains a problem he may be having, the associate is *not* going to say, "Well, that's not my department. Let me transfer you." Not after just saying, "Welcome to the World's Greatest Bank."

Early on we had customers who couldn't believe we were serious and asked, "What makes you think you're the world's greatest bank? And I'd reply, "Bottom line, you have us. Every one of us is committed to taking total responsibility for our customers and making sure we do things right." I'll admit we stubbed our toes along the way as we improved our service, but I think our customers quickly sensed that we were sincere.

As Neal notes, when we first started calling ourselves "The World's Greatest Bank" in 1996, a lot of people didn't think we were serious. We had less than a dozen stores then and our competitors, some of whom were ten times our size, scoffed at us for calling ourselves "The World's Greatest Bank." They made fun of us. Not anymore! Not after more than ten years of relentless growth—which, by the way, included acquiring some of those same competitors!

Neal put up the first banner in 1996. "The World's Greatest Bank" was adopted as the vision for the company by the board in 2000, and that's when the standard was applied throughout the company to *become* the world's greatest bank. Everybody started answering the phones, "Welcome to The World's Greatest Bank." Since then we have put up "The World's Greatest Bank" signs in all our stores.

I think our experience illustrates a number of crucial lessons.

Don't worry if your vision sounds corny, unrealistic, or unreasonable. The people who count, who see you as their leader, will not think your vision is corny or unreasonable unless they also think it is just a bunch of words—if they sense that you are not absolutely committed and passionate about achieving your vision or that you don't have the discipline to live your vision day in and day out. As a slogan, a bunch of words, "The World's Greatest Bank" *is* corny. But for us it's not an advertising slogan. We don't use it in marketing at all. We do it for *ourselves*. It represents our state of mind. It's what we stand for, what we confidently aspire to become, what we optimistically believe we can achieve. "The World's Greatest Bank" is a call to action, *a standard that we set for ourselves.* In that light, it's not unreasonable at all.

Suppose we had listened to conventional wisdom that a small regional bank could never be the world's greatest bank. Suppose we decided to be *reasonable* and settled for a smaller vision: say, "A Pretty Good Bank in the Pacific Northwest." We would not have achieved anywhere near the dedication, commitment, and passion we have in our company, qualities that are living parts of our culture, qualities that have propelled our extraordinary growth.

> Give your people unreasonable goals, because unreasonable goals inspire people to reach for a higher level.

Too many companies use committees to craft vision statements that turn into strings of platitudes. You know the type: *We will ethically pursue excellence in all that we do.* Pretty bland.

It takes a contagious level of passion to inspire people to exceed their expectations of themselves. Give your people unreasonable goals, because unreasonable goals inspire people to reach for a higher level. As Gary Hamel says in *Leading the Revolution,* "Modest aspirations beget incrementalism. . . . Only when people subscribe to unreasonable goals will they start searching for breakthrough ideas."

Never, not for one moment, let yourself worry about being perceived as unreasonable.

Passion Starts at the Top

Read almost any business book and you'll see talk about the value of passion and how important it is to hire people who are passionate about the company's work or mission. And that is certainly true, as Neal's story demonstrates. (I will talk about getting the right people—which includes the capacity for this kind of focus—on the bus in Chapter Twelve.) But make no mistake, like discipline, *passion starts at the top.*

I don't think you can manufacture passion. It's something you find, or more often, something that finds *you*. Bill George, who was CEO of Medtronic for many years, took a long time to find his passion. In *Authentic Leadership*, George talks about his search for passion at work. "It took me twenty years in business to find the right place to devote my energies—a mission-driven company named Medtronic." He talks about how unfulfilling it was, in spite of promotions and much success, to work for a company he couldn't feel passionate about. The key to fulfillment as a leader, he writes, is to find "a purpose that ignites your passion." He adds:

> Throughout my life I have had a passion to make a difference in the world. . . . I feel a deep sense of good fortune in finding a confluence of interests between my personal desires and the needs of Medtronic. The Medtronic mission to restore people to fuller health inspired me from the moment Medtronic founder Earl Bakken described it to me. Fourteen years later, it inspires me even more.

With passion work can be a heroic quest.

If you, the leader, don't have passion for your vision of the company, you cannot expect others to. Work without passion is just a job; with passion work can be a heroic quest. If you don't see yourself and your company as embarked on a heroic quest—pursuing something you are really passionate about, something that makes challenges and heartache worthwhile—you really should rethink what you're doing and where you're going.

If we hadn't developed the discipline to live up to everything "The World's Greatest Bank" stands for, it would have been the joke our competitors first thought it was. But if we didn't also have *passion* and *optimism* to fuel our quest, I'm sure we would have burned ourselves out long ago.

Spread the Passion

At Umpqua we have developed many ways to inspire passion, including our motivational moments, our Celebration of Excellence Awards, our Town Hall meetings, our World's Greatest Bank

University, and many others. I'll get back to these in later chapters. Here I want to focus on the specific role of a leader: how you personally can spread the passion.

Passion is only good in business if you share it with your people. The best way I know of to inspire passion in people is *to be passionate about them*. Let them feel the love! They are the ones who are going the extra miles to translate vision into reality. Treat them like the heroes you want them to be! You have to be passionate about your people, passionate about helping them succeed. If you're not passionate about your people, I don't think you can really be passionate about your vision—not unless you're delusional enough to think it is all up to you.

I see my job as head of support. If I don't support the people under me, we fail. Simple as that. It starts with me. If I'm not the head cheerleader, shouting myself hoarse to encourage the team, forget it! Too many CEOs retreat to their ivory tower and lose touch. I think that is the beginning of the end. I'm always out and about, seeing what's happening, learning from people, listening to their problems, sharing my vision and what I'm trying to do. If you want your company to grow, get out there with your people.

I maintain an open door policy. Anybody in the company can drop by to talk to me or pick up the phone and call me. You can't lead people and be in a cocoon. You've got to be accessible. How else can you lead people? I've seen too many CEOs who try to lead by remote control and it doesn't work. If I'm in a meeting in my office with an important client and I spot an associate walking by who looks in, sees that I'm in a meeting, and keeps going, I'll excuse myself and walk out. "Hey, you need me?"

"I wanted to ask you a question," the passer-by might say.

"Well, go ahead. You're important to me."

The client usually doesn't care. In fact, most of the time they're impressed because they see how much I care about my people. I make sure my people know that they are important to me.

You've got to let your people know you care. If someone in your company is facing a family crisis, such as a serious illness, be there for them. I had a top manager whose father was extremely ill and he said he needed to take some time off. I said, "You take all the time you want. You take care of your family. Don't worry about the bank; we're going to be around. You take care of your family. Don't worry about us; we're going to worry about *you*."

Loyalty to my people is part of my style—maybe to a fault. A common problem executives have is to hang on too long to people who aren't going to make it. I try not to do that, but I'm sure I have. But for people who are trying their best, I have an incredible amount of loyalty. I will give them the benefit of the doubt every single time. But if you aren't trying your best, you're gone; I'm not going to mess with you. I'm loyal to people who are singing our song.

It's the passion that gets you up every day. And that's what has to be communicated to your people. If you communicate your passion effectively people will quickly understand what the corporate values are, what the heart and soul of the company is, and what the culture is ultimately going to become. You have to tell them what it is again and again and then set the example by doing it. Live up to what you say it is. If you set expectations, you have to live up to those expectations yourself. Visiting the troops is part of that with my company. I can't do it enough. I get up close and personal to allow them to see the whites of my eyes regarding my commitment.

> I allow them to see the whites of my eyes.

As you think about this chapter and its themes of passion, optimism, and unreasonable expectations, I want to leave you with this bit from *Alice in Wonderland:*

"One can't believe impossible things," Alice tells the White Queen. "I daresay you haven't had much practice," the Queen replies. "When I was your age, I always did it for half-an-hour a day. Why, sometimes I've believed as many as six impossible things before breakfast."

MOTIVATIONAL MOMENT
What's in Your Briefcase?

Exercise: Distribute sheets with the briefcase drawing (below). Tell the group, "Identify three to five intangible things you will carry in your briefcase today to make it great! Draw or write each item in the briefcase drawing.

"When your briefcase is full, share with the rest of the group."

MY BRIEFCASE

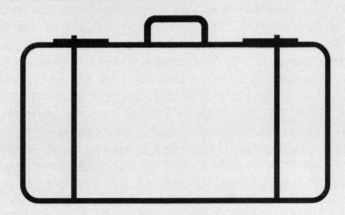

You pack your own briefcase each and every day. What you choose to carry with you is up to you—make it filled with optimism and passion!
—Ray

Chapter 4

Snap the Rubber Band Syndrome

I believe that each of us has a rubber band with one end attached to our backside and the other nailed firmly to the wall of tradition. Even when we want to change, and *do* change, we tend to relax and the rubber band snaps us back into our comfort zones.

The rubber band syndrome is what is responsible for the yo-yo weight loss and gain found among struggling dieters. Once they shed those pounds, they think they can relax and soon the rubber band of habit pulls them back to where they were before the diet. People who successfully lose weight *and keep it off* never go off their diet, although they may modify it. They don't achieve their goal of losing twenty pounds and decide to celebrate with pizza and ice cream. They don't think, "Great! Now I can go back to the way I was eating before."

The rubber band syndrome shows up in all aspects of life, whether we are trying to lose weight, save money, stop smoking, or raise our children differently. And we don't escape the rubber band syndrome just because we go to work.

When you are leading your company for growth, you know you are going to disrupt comfortable routines and ask for new behavior, new priorities, new skills. When you try to stretch your people, I promise you, you are going to run into the same rubber band syndrome. People will, most of them anyway, get with the new program initially, but if you don't keep an eye out, the rubber band will snap them back to the wall of tradition before long. This can paralyze leadership and the people who make up your company.

As I told the board of South Umpqua State Bank when they recruited me in 1994, I was interested in coming on board only if they wanted wholesale change that would create shareholder value. The leader's job is to get people *used to change,* so used to it that the elasticity of the rubber band is stretched too far to retain its power to pull people back to their comfort zone even if it is where they want to go! Change is a constant in today's world. We all have to adapt to it.

If we don't learn to live with change, we have to realize we may not be around very long. Army Chief of Staff General Eric Shinseki understood this very well. Two years before 9/11, the army decided to transform itself—leaving behind the armor-heavy structures designed to fight the Soviet Union to become lighter, more flexible, and more rapidly deployable. Of course, the army is one of the most tradition-bound organizations around, and General Shinseki faced a barrage of resistance and criticism. But he had a clear warning for the officers who objected to the transformation process. "If you don't like change, you're going to like irrelevance even less," Shinseki told them. "The army must change because the nation cannot afford to have an army that is irrelevant." Businesses that can't change don't just become irrelevant, they become *extinct.*

Tradition has two sides, one good and one bad. The good side of tradition is that it can be the glue that holds things together and provides esprit de corps. The bad side is that it is the glue that prevents the leader from changing outdated rules. I believe that companies need to honor their traditions. But don't let traditions become your company's tar pit! Honor them—and know when to let go.

One of my board members, David Frohnmayer, who is president of the University of Oregon, once told me, "We're in a world of permanent whitewater. There aren't any sections of slow water. We're not moving from one pool to another. We've had to constantly renavigate and reorient ourselves."

I know I am going to catch hell for saying this, but sometimes I find it useful to change things around *just to change things around*—just to keep people on their toes so they don't get set in their ways. Good athletes are always on their toes, knees bent, alert, and watchful. Even when standing still, they aren't really still, they're shifting their weight from foot to foot. They are ready to

> If you want your company to be a relentless growth machine, you've got to train people to be used to change, expect change, adjust to change, and even welcome change.

move, and move quickly, depending on the demands of the action. Good athletes are never caught flat-footed, and they train constantly to stay sharp. It's the same in business. You want people to stay sharp, and you have to train them to get used to change, to be ready for change at a moment's notice. Then if something urgent comes up, your company won't be caught flat-footed. If you want your company to be a relentless growth machine, you've got to train people to be used to change, expect change, adjust to change, and even welcome change.

How to Snap the Rubber Band

Umpqua was a small bank that had been around for forty-some years when I arrived; some of the employees had been with the company for twenty years or more. So you can imagine they were used to doing the same things over and over. We had to break the paradigm of "this is the way we do things." You've got to lure people outside their secure comfort zones, loosen their rubber bands. Here are some of the things I found effective.

Get Them Excited

When I first started reinventing Umpqua, both people in the bank and interested outsiders told me we were going to lose at least a third of the employees. The conventional wisdom was that people so set in their ways would be very resistant to trying new things. But the interesting thing is that we lost very few people. Some of the old-timers were among the best advocates for what I was trying to achieve. They had been waiting for a sense of direction. Their attitude was, "Get us excited, for goodness sake."

I wonder why so many people treat *change* as a four-letter word. *Change* is not a four-letter word! People who fear change think of nightmare events like a monster under the bed. Change can sometimes be bad, but it can also be extraordinarily great and inspiring. I have always thought that change could mean good things, wonderful things: the satisfaction of personal growth, the security of prosperity, the joy of accomplishment, the pride of building something significant. Life is all about change: just watch your children grow up. We sometimes fantasize, wishing we could freeze time and keep our precious children with us forever, but we would never really want that. Change is a positive force.

Change is perceived as either good or bad, there's not much of a middle ground. There's no Door Number Three, as I said earlier. And if the rules are that change is either good or bad, then it behooves us as leaders to present change as good—and if you are leading for growth, then change should be good. Executives who can instill in their people the sense that change should be viewed as positive have completed a significant step toward reaching their goals. Inspired people thinking positively can accomplish miracles. When people look at change as a positive, they take your idea and make it better.

> Get people excited about change and they'll welcome it.

In Chapter Three I emphasized the importance of positive passion. If you are optimistic and passionate about your company's future, your people will be too. People may be comfortable with old routines, but they also find them boring. Nobody wants to spend forty-plus hours a week being bored. Get people excited about change and they'll welcome it.

Offer Full Disclosure

If I'm alone in my house at night and I hear a noise upstairs, I think, *What was that?* It makes me nervous. But if I go upstairs and find out it was a book I left on the edge of the bed that just fell off, that's that. You can deal with things you know. Things you don't know can scare the hell out of you. You can let your imagination go wild: that noise upstairs could have been an axe murderer!

Whether they like it or not, leaders have the power to scare the hell out of people. If you don't fully explain what you are up to, you leave people in the dark, and people in the dark have vivid imaginations. They might not imagine you're an axe murderer, but I can assure you, they will imagine something close. And when people are afraid, they shut down right away and don't hear what you have to say. So if you want your people to get excited about change, you sure shouldn't scare them. You've got to give people information, and lots of it, so they don't wonder what is really going on and start imagining all sorts of worst-case scenarios.

> Leaders have the power to scare the hell out of people.

I always tell my people, I owe you an explanation of what we're doing. Here's what we're doing, why we're doing it, what we hope to achieve, and most important, how we are going to support you as we implement the changes. When people know the full story, you'll be amazed at how accepting and supportive they can be.

I believe that leaders do not have to defend their actions. However, all leaders should be able to explain their actions. There is no point in getting defensive. I think this is one of the biggest mistakes executives make: they don't want to put themselves in a position where they have to defend their actions, so they avoid explaining them in the first place. This isn't fair to their people and it ultimately undermines the leaders' own efforts.

Make Them Accountable

I already talked about this at length in Chapter Two. The quickest way to demonstrate to people that you are serious about new changes is to hold them accountable. Executives must monitor and hold their people accountable for adhering to the new strategies that are being employed. If they do, something very interesting happens. People will want inspection—or, to put it differently, will want to demonstrate to their superiors and peers how much they support the new initiatives. Remember the woman I told you about who sent me that e-mail? She wanted me to come and see how she was doing. She wanted to be measured and held accountable. These people are what I call "keepers."

Support Them

When you ask people to try something new or do things differently, you're really asking them to take a risk. They might fail. That's what stepping outside your comfort zone is all about. You wouldn't ask someone with no acrobatic experience to walk across a high wire with no training, support, or safety net. It's the same in business.

I have what I call "focus groups" for our associates. These aren't the focus groups with one-way mirrors that marketing people do with customers: these are for employees so that I can focus on what they need from me. I hold these frequently in all different parts of the company, in different geographical regions and functional areas. I tell them, "I need to hear from you guys. If we're going to make this company better, I need to know where we need to improve. And if our new initiatives aren't working as well as we planned, I need to know what we can do to turn things around. So I need your constructive criticism." It cuts right through the layers of management that can keep information from the CEO.

When I conduct a focus group with frontline associates, I never have their managers present. (One rule I follow during these sessions is never to talk about people issues that arise between them and their supervisors. All other topics are on the table.) I want to hear from people directly, and I want people to hear directly from me. We usually discuss a process, procedure, policy, or a needed piece of equipment. Half the issues that come up I can fix right away, which makes me wonder why somebody else didn't already take care of it. And the other 50 percent I push back to people to look at immediately. But the point is, they know I'm looking out for them. I'm not sending them out on a high wire with no support or safety net.

Act Like a Human Being

When you are leading people, it is always good to remember that you are one. If you set yourself up on a pedestal as superhuman, even infallible, people are going to be itching to knock you down. If you remember that you are a human being who can't do it all alone, people will have a whole different attitude.

One of my favorite sayings is, "Give me the benefit of the doubt." I tell this to my people all the time. If you ask anyone who has been at Umpqua for a length of time for a catchphrase they associate with me, they'll probably tell you, "Ray's always asking us to give him the benefit of the doubt." I use it mostly when I'm trying to start a new initiative, especially if it goes against the conventional wisdom. And it is really helpful in getting people to move ahead. What does this tell people? First, it tells them that I recognize that people do have doubts. I don't expect to have a bunch of true believers following me around like zombies. But I do expect them to give me the benefit of the doubt and make a real effort. Second, I'm not setting myself up as all-knowing: if I knew exactly how it was going to work out, I could just issue the plan and that would be that. Third, we are all going to work on this together— we are all going to figure it out together. Fourth, perhaps most important, I'm opening myself up, admitting I don't know all the answers, and asking for help. It's amazing how responsive people can be when you genuinely and sincerely ask for their help.

The next time you are trying to persuade the people in your company to break away from conventional wisdom and take a risk on something new, try it. Say, "Give me the benefit of the doubt."

Don't Manage Change—Lead It

When I hear people talk about managing a change project, I cringe. Change is not a project like implementing a new management information system. When you talk about a change *project*, it implies you expect to have a beginning, a middle, and an end, when you can declare okay, the project's over, "We've changed!" John Kotter, whose book *Leading Change* has many valuable lessons, says that a common error in leading change is "declaring victory too soon." I hate to disagree, but I think he is wrong. The big mistake is declaring victory at all. Once you declare victory, you're telling people they've arrived. They can let down their guard. And then the rubber band syndrome slowly starts to pull them back. If you *ever* declare victory, it is too soon.

> If you *ever* declare victory, it is too soon.

The other thing that bothers me about managing change is in that word *managing*. I suppose you can manage some types of change: downsizing, restructuring, and similar difficult challenges. But when you are talking about growing your company, fulfilling your vision of the future, you can't manage that type of change. You must lead it.

To my way of thinking, if you are a leader who really believes in the direction of the organization, who has the positive passion discussed in Chapter Three, then you are going to be in the trenches with people at all levels of the organization, learning and changing along with them—leading them through the change.

I think too many leaders take change for granted. They delegate it to the next level and walk away. When they come back, they find that the results weren't what they expected. You can't delegate the vision for your company. Most of all, you can't delegate leadership. As I said before, you cannot lead people by remote control.

MOTIVATIONAL MOMENT
Moving Forward

Exercise: Have the people you're working with sit on chairs with wheels. Ask them to roll their chairs backward, ten feet or so. Now ask them to move their chairs forward (while still facing forward).

Comment: It is really easy to go backwards and do things the way they have "always" been done. Moving forward is much more challenging, but you will continually grow and experience new and exciting things.

Chapter 5

What's Going On Behind Your Back?

One more prerequisite must be in place before you stand a good chance of leading your company on a path of relentless growth. Let's assume you have figured out what business you are really in and developed your game plan; you have made sure you have the self-discipline to stay true to your plan in the face of conventional wisdom and other obstacles; you have also generated the positive passion that comes from a clear vision of your future, and you have snapped the rubber band syndrome and made clear to your people that you are personally involved in leading them through the changes ahead. None of that will get you very far if you don't have the ability to find out what's going on behind your back, on the ground. Are your strategies being implemented effectively? If not, you are going to go nowhere in a hurry.

The only way I know of to find out what's going on behind my back is to have other people tell me. I can't be everywhere at once. And I don't have eyes in the back of my head. I need other people to watch my back. You can walk around all day with a piece of toilet paper trailing you if no one is willing to tell you, "Hey, you've got some paper stuck to your shoe."

> You can walk around all day with a piece of toilet paper trailing you if no one is willing to tell you the truth.

Some leaders think metrics will tell them what is going on behind their backs. Now metrics are fine for giving you a snapshot of how your business is doing. You can measure productivity, return on investment, quarterly financial results, and much more. In fact, you can even measure intangible things like quality, as Umpqua does. (I'll tell you about our Return on Quality program in Chapter Fourteen.) And those sorts of metrics are important. But they only measure results. They tell you where you've been and how far you've come. But they don't provide real-time feedback. They don't help you watch your back.

Make People Feel Safe in Telling the Truth

Let me share a message I recently received from one of our associates. It came in after I made a broadcast telephone call to all the associates of the bank. I do broadcast calls, which allow associates to dial into a central phone number quarterly for regular updates and at times when we have big news to report. This particular call announced our deal to acquire Western Sierra Bank, considerably strengthening our presence in the Northern California market. Shortly after the call, I received this e-mail:

> From: XXXX
>
> Date: Wed Feb 08 10:24:07
>
> To: Ray Davis
>
> Re: Confidential
>
> Just want to share my thoughts with you about the broadcast call this morning. I understand you must be exhausted and it showed. I missed hearing you "talk" to us about the news—the excitement and passion were missing. Having you read details about the new banks seemed impersonal. For all of us who know what's in store for the next several months, we wanted the message to be "we're in this together and we know how to do it right. . . . "
>
> Sorry—hopefully you will appreciate my honesty. I know you have many, many meetings ahead in the next few weeks where you will be in front of associates—many who are a bit anxious about a merger. They need to see your passion.
>
> Thanks for listening. See you next week.

I've gone on for several pages telling you about the importance of passion and here was someone in the ranks telling me I wasn't showing enough passion!

What *courage* that took!

I e-mailed her right back and thanked her. Now, I think the conference call went fine. That's *my* perception. But she felt I let her down—that's *her* perception, which is a lot more important. I followed up a few days later with a phone call. I said, "I want to thank you for expressing yourself to me. Every now and then, maybe I need a reminder too to fill my tank and get fired up. Thanks for the reminder. I promise you I'll do better."

I have known my e-mail correspondent for quite a while. When the company was smaller we worked closely together, though as the company grew our roles diverged. But I wasn't upset that she had sent me a critical e-mail. I would have been upset if she had felt that way and kept it to herself, not telling me. That would have meant that somewhere along the way the trust had gone out of our relationship. It would have meant that I had work to do to rebuild our relationship.

The point I'm trying to make is that you won't know what is going on behind your back if you don't make it safe for your people to tell you things, especially things they think you may not want to hear. It comes down to a simple question: Are you trustworthy? Can your people trust you not to fly off the handle when they tell you the truth?

As a leader, you are utterly dependent on people providing you with the information you need. You can get a lot of information yourself with your own eyes and ears, of course, but that only goes so far. You can order up reports, but reports and PowerPoint presentations are usually so worked over that insight and telling details are baked out of them. And as I said, metrics only tell you where you've been.

Do your people feel safe when they talk to you? Or do they clam up when you walk by? If people don't trust you enough to tell you the truth, you've got a lot of work to do.

The same day that I got that e-mail, I had a meeting with several hundred associates of the bank we had just acquired. I was telling them about our culture, the Umpqua culture, and emphasizing that it was very different from most corporate cultures. They asked for examples. So I read that e-mail. And I asked them what would happen in most companies if someone sent an e-mail like that to the CEO or another executive. "Oh," they said, "they'd be in deep trouble or out the door."

"Not at Umpqua!" I roared back. That's the difference in how we run our company. That's how we make sure leaders at all levels know what is going on behind their backs.

You need to hear the bad news, and you need to make it safe for people to tell you the bad news.

Many business books will tell you that the secret of good leadership is "communicate, communicate, communicate!" Well, here's an even bigger secret: *Listen, Listen, Listen!* And you need to listen not just to people in your executive team, but to people at all levels of your company.

I expect my executives to have the same sense of urgency that I have when it comes to our staff, our people. When that breaks down, I can get really upset with them. Recently, I was talking to a guy who runs a division in the company and he informed me that one of his people had recently left the bank.

I asked him why.

He said that the woman who left the bank felt that the backroom activities were getting to be too much like a big bank, and were making it cumbersome for her to generate the documents needed for mortgage loans. She felt she could actually make more money at a smaller bank, where there wouldn't be so many hurdles. That was a real red flag for me. I tell everyone that we have to guard against "big bank creep" setting in. So I asked him, "Why did she feel that we were acting like a big bank?"

He said, "Well, Ray, I just don't know."

I just about lost it right then and there. I said, "If you don't know, who the hell am I supposed to ask? And why didn't *you* ask her? Why wouldn't you sit her down and talk to her before she leaves? The issue may have been something you could have corrected right on the spot. If she was good at her job, why wouldn't you do that?" He admitted that he probably should have.

Those are the sorts of things that drive me crazy. You've got to encourage everyone on your team to take enough interest in their people to ask questions and listen. You can't know what's going on behind your back if your executives and managers don't know what's going on behind *their* backs.

You Need to Be Able to Trust Your People

The other side of making people feel safe in telling the truth, of course, is that you must absolutely demand the truth from your people. People need to feel safe in telling you the truth, but they should be very afraid to shade the truth or to tell an outright lie. Your people have an absolute right to trust in you. By the same token, you need to be able to trust your people.

I had one top executive (I'll call him Bob) who, I realize in hindsight, had never bought in to what we were trying to do with the bank, the idea that we were really in the retail services business. Of course, to my face Bob would tell me exactly what I wanted to hear (which should have been a tip-off right there). But behind my back, he made it clear to others that he did not agree with what I was trying to do and ridiculed many of the things that made Umpqua unique, like our motivational moments. Because I had made it safe for people to talk to me, I soon found out that he was being two-faced with me. He didn't really deserve my trust, but unfortunately, I let it slide.

> Your people have an absolute right to trust in you. By the same token, you need to be able to trust your people.

As leaders, we all recognize that we are going to get a certain amount of "happy talk" and insincere flattery. People try to fool us. But most of the time, *we try to fool ourselves.* Sometimes we give people too much rope. We don't cut the cord as quickly as we should. And sad to say, one of the reasons is our own convenience. We don't want to go through the disruption and trouble of moving someone in a key position out of the organization and finding someone new. We tell ourselves, "I know this guy's game. I can deal with him." We think to ourselves, "I'll turn him around."

In fact, what you're doing is hurting everything you stand for. Your reputation is being hurt in the eyes of the staff. They see someone undercutting the values and strategies you are trying to

> ## Most of the time, we try to fool ourselves.

promote, and they wonder why you aren't doing something about it.

When you have a guy saying all the right things, being a real cheerleader, and you realize deep down that his heart is just not in it, that you can't trust him, don't let it slide. Take action.

With Bob, things finally came to a head. I heard stories from the field about another person I'll call Sam, whom Bob had recently hired and who reported directly to Bob. I investigated and found that Sam was abusing people verbally. He would go into people's offices and threaten them: "If you don't do what I say, I'll fire you." He was managing by intimidation, which is totally against our values. We treat people fairly. Once I collected enough information, I acted as fast as I could. I got both Sam and Bob in the room. I told Sam, "I am going to warn you right now. I am going to tell you some things I've learned, and if you try to argue with me, I'm going to terminate you on the spot. I want you to sit there and listen to me." And I went into great detail about things I knew he was doing and told him that if he didn't stop immediately, he was fired. He had the good sense not to argue.

At the end of the meeting I told him I wanted a plan on my desk in five days showing specifically how he was going to remedy the damage he'd caused and the ordeal he'd put people through. Normally, I told him, when people do these sorts of things, their reputation is hurt so badly that they can't dig themselves out of the hole they just dug. "And if it doesn't look like you can dig yourself out, I'll tell you. Or you can decide right now that you can't and leave."

He assured me he didn't want to leave, he wanted to fix things, to make amends and repair the damage. He promised I would have the action plan in five days and left.

Then I turned to Bob, and asked him, "Why am I here? Sam doesn't work for me." I went on, "He works for you and you've known what he was up to. If I have to do your job for you, I don't need you. This is basic Management 101. But the real issue is, how could you support our values as you say you do and let Sam treat people that way? I thought we were walking side by side, working together to build the bank. But if you don't buy in to how we do things around here, especially in treating our associates fairly, then you don't belong here."

I didn't actually fire Bob on the spot, but he saw the handwriting on the wall, and shortly thereafter he decided to leave the bank. Sam did submit his plan and did get better, but after a while—remember the rubber band syndrome—he reverted to his old behavior and I had to terminate him. It was, no doubt, a year too late.

As I've said, we try to fool ourselves. I sure did with these two. And I did a disservice to my staff, who had to put up with them for months, listening to them badmouth not only me but all the things we were trying to do.

Well, I hope I've learned my lesson. I'll try not to fool myself again, thinking I can work with people who are not 100 percent trustworthy. Yes, you often have to cut people some slack—but not when it comes to honesty and trust issues.

Happy Talk

I mentioned earlier that leaders have to expect a certain amount of happy talk from their people. It's not unknown, however, for leaders to engage in happy talk themselves. Leaders have to project optimism, but they also have to tell it like it is. Empty happy talk and rosy scenarios unconnected to reality can only undermine trust and confidence in a leader.

Sometimes leaders don't give people enough credit. People know when you are jerking them around. When executives try to take the easy way out and say what they think people want to hear, the people they're talking to sense it. Of course, some leaders straight out lie, but most don't. Still, they don't go all out with the truth either. If it's a difficult issue, they'll often try to kick it down the road. They'll tell you what they think you want to hear to make you feel better or to make you go away for now, but they have no intention of following up. They don't see themselves as lying to people. They think they've bought themselves some time; they'll deal with it when they get the new supervisor on board or when the current crisis passes. They aren't specifically lying, but they're not giving out the whole nine yards. And they lose credibility.

The quickest way you can undermine the practice of telling the truth is not to tell the unvarnished truth yourself. That should go without saying.

Just the Tip of the Iceberg

The long and short of all this is that if you want to know what is going on behind your back so that you can make sure your strategy is being implemented effectively—and the values your strategy requires are being honored—you need to promote a culture of truth telling. You must make sure people feel safe in telling the truth. Those who can't or won't tell the truth must be weeded out of the organization.

The key points I've discussed in this chapter are just the tip of the iceberg in ensuring that you know what is going on behind your back. You need to find many vehicles to allow information to flow to you, and put systems in place that generate the information you need. I discuss these later in the book.

 MOTIVATIONAL MOMENT
What's on Your Back?

Exercise: Participants take turns taping a blank piece of paper on one another's backs. Then everyone circulates around writing positive qualities about each person on the paper, words such as *leader, humorous, hard-working,* and the like.

Conclusion: Each participant has a list of compliments from other members of the team.

We all need people to help us watch our backs!
    —Ray

Part Two

Roles of a Leader

Once you've put the prerequisites in place in your company, you've laid the groundwork to become a relentless competitor. Critical leadership tasks remain. This part of the book describes the decisive aspects of leading and managing that have to start at the top if they are to start anywhere. As I see it, you have five roles to fill in leading for growth:

Support your people—and hold them accountable. Leaders have many roles, but I think these two are critical and they go hand in hand. Leaders have to be the champions of the people on the front lines, making sure they have the training and tools they need to deliver results. And at the same time, leaders need to hold their people accountable for delivering results.

Empower your people by giving them permission to make decisions. Management experts have been discussing empowerment for years, but before you skip this chapter, ask yourself if you are really satisfied that the people who work for you feel secure in making decisions. I explain how to tell if your people are genuinely empowered and describe how setting "foul lines" can make it safe for people to make decisions.

Take yourself out of the daily fray to rise above the battlefield. Leaders need to know what is happening on the front lines, but they also need a strategic perspective on the company and where it is going. I explain the tactics I use to transcend the day-to-day details and—just as important—how I help the people on my executive team do this as well.

Explain your vision. Leaders cannot delegate the job of explaining their vision for the company—what I call "this movie that's playing in my head." It is not just a matter of articulating the vision; the leader must demonstrate the vision by living it every single day.

Be yourself. Leading is hard work. It can be exhausting. And you can't do it well while you're pretending to be someone else. If you can't be yourself, you can't lead. It's as simple as that.

Chapter 6

Support Your People—
and Hold 'Em Accountable

Good ideas or strategies really work only if they get better once you turn them over to others. In other words, once you turn your back on them they must get better if they are going to be sustainable. If they don't take on a life of their own and improve, they usually die—and most of the time it will be a fast death. Once you move on to other initiatives, do the ideas that you have turned over to others slow down or become less effective? Or do they move faster due to an inspired workforce that has the tools and resources they need to take your ideas and improve on them?

At Umpqua, our strategy for growth was to shift the playing field, to compete with other banks on our own terms, not theirs. As I described in Chapter One, we figured we could differentiate ourselves from the bland sameness infecting the banking industry and attract customers by seeing ourselves as a retailer and providing a superior customer experience. It turned out to be a pretty good strategy. But having the right strategy would have gotten us nowhere unless everyone in the bank embraced ownership of it and we executed it almost flawlessly at all levels.

If you want to lead for growth, you must first understand that coming up with an idea for a new process, product, or store design that gives you a competitive edge is really the easy part. As they say, good ideas are a dime a dozen. What separates the winners from the also-rans is the ability to take a good idea *and make it work.*

That's execution—and that's the hard part.

In *Leading the Revolution,* Gary Hamel writes about "competitive gaps," innovations that companies create to separate themselves

What separates the winners from the also-rans is the ability to take a good idea *and* *make it work.*

from their competitors. Over time, competitive gaps evaporate as competitors catch up. Umpqua first created a competitive gap with our original concept store in Roseburg, opened in 1996. To make sure our advantage remained fresh and did not gradually evaporate, we felt we needed to continue to innovate around this store and also to develop a next-generation store, which we opened in the Pearl District, a renovated area of boutiques, restaurants, and night clubs in downtown Portland.

I like to think that we took the great retail ideas of our Roseburg store and added science to create the store now known as the Pearl (Figure 6.1). Our science provider was an international design

FIGURE 6.1   UMPQUA'S PEARL STORE

firm called Ziba. This store included all the elements of the original Roseburg store (improved and updated 100 percent) plus new merchandizing techniques that appeal to all five senses. We pay attention not only to what people see, but also to what they hear, smell (fresh coffee), taste (we provide chocolates with every transaction), and touch.

Today and over the last ten years bankers have come from all over the world to see how Umpqua has successfully differentiated itself. However, after they see how the Pearl and Umpqua's other stores operate they quickly start asking questions about how we get our people to serve our customers in the manner that they do.

"Ray," they'll say, "your store is pretty, but how do you get your people to interact like that with your customers?"

That's the hard part. It's more than coming up with a good strategy or designing a fancy store. It's about flawless execution on the ground, day in and day out. That's really how we differentiate ourselves from all the other banks.

So how did we get our people to act like that? We supported them and held them accountable.

Don't Fall in Love with Your Title

If you're a president or CEO or senior vice president, no doubt you worked hard to earn that position. And yes, your title gives you a certain amount of authority. But it doesn't tell you what is really important—it doesn't tell you what your job really is.

My title is president and CEO, and that's the title I use when I'm out in public representing the company or when I'm on the phone talking about our quarterly results with Wall Street analysts. But when I'm talking to our people, I tell them to scratch out "President and CEO" on my business card and write in "Head of Support," which is my real title in their eyes. I've mentioned this before in passing, but I'm bringing it up again because it really is important. If you're serious about growing your company and your growth strategies are working, then no doubt things are moving along at a good clip. You've got more business today than you did yesterday, and you've got ambitious targets that you expect to meet tomorrow. Your people have more to do today than they did yesterday and in many ways their jobs today are different from yesterday's. In a fast-paced growth environment like this, you have simply got to support your people or you're heading for a crash. When people are supported, on the other hand, they can take your ideas and make them better. They can even increase the tempo and propel your company ahead even faster.

So I really do see my job as head of support, to provide our people with the tools and the training they need to do their jobs at the standards we've set within the company. Because things are moving so quickly, I can't assume that the tools and support that worked yesterday will be sufficient today. I'm out there all the time, asking, "What is it you need?" It's a constant. It's the only way we can keep up with our own growth.

Support involves much more than training. Of course you've got to provide training in specific skills and tasks, but that is just the beginning. Do your people have the systems they need? Do they have problem-solving resources they can turn to when something goes wrong? Do policies and procedures help them do their jobs or—as is so often the case—simply present extra hurdles they need to jump over before they can do their jobs? And most important, do they have the decision-making authority they need to achieve results? I am always out there asking these questions. What can I do for you? What is it you need? What type of decision-making authority do you need to provide the level of service that Umpqua is so well known for?

Providing the tools isn't just a matter of giving people a standardized bag of goodies, training, or equipment. Most likely, any resources you've offered long enough to standardize are already getting outdated. But more important, they don't meet people's individual needs. That's why you've got to ask people directly what they need.

A widespread belief in management is that you've got to treat people the same. You shouldn't make individual exceptions. I think that is dead wrong. I got a call once from an executive. One of the loan officers reporting to him was asking for a special kind of support that we had never considered before. He wanted us to pay for his membership in an exclusive club where he could meet with and entertain customers. The executive told me that this loan officer (I'll call him Ernie) was a star performer. His results were head-and-shoulders above every other loan officer's. The executive raved about him, but was worried that since no one else had this sort of perk, he would have to give it to everybody if he let Ernie have it. He thought he had to treat everybody the same.

My advice was to give Ernie the membership. Some would consider it a perk, but it was really a tool he could use to generate business. I told the executive, "Not only should you give Ernie the membership, you should also ask, 'Is there *anything else* you need?' When the other loan officers come to you and ask why Ernie got the membership, you can tell them that when they've achieved the numbers Ernie has, they can have the membership too." It puts pressure on the person rewarded, because he's got to continue to perform, and it puts pressure on the others, because if they want it, they have to earn it. This really surprised the executive, who thought we couldn't make exceptions for people. Of course, that is no reason not to give people the support they need. When people are exceptional, you must make exceptions for them.

> When people are exceptional, you must make exceptions for them.

Have a Sense of Urgency

When dealing with the troops, a manager must communicate a sense of urgency. When people ask for a specific tool or another form of support, you can't say you'll look into it and then put it on the back burner until you find the time to deal with it. Not if you want your company to keep growing. Most requests for support are very simple, and management just needs the self-discipline to sit down and deliver. So I try to instill that sense of urgency in myself and my top execs: if people in the field make a reasonable request, we respond right away. It's a matter of showing the people who work for us that they are important. If we didn't feel that way, we wouldn't do a lot of the things we do.

I tell my people that if something is a big deal to you, it's a bigger deal to me. I want them to speak up and let us know *right away* when something becomes an issue. Because if something is affecting one person, it's probably bothering a lot of other people.

I've mentioned our Town Hall meetings, which we hold every quarter. People can send in their questions and complaints anonymously. However they are written, that's how we read them. We don't edit out anything. At a recent Town Hall meeting, I got this comment:

> I've sent in question to PulsePoint [a feature on our intranet where associates can send in their questions, complaints, and suggestions for improvement, and we make sure to address them] and got a quick response saying that my comment had been forwarded on to [Executive X] and I appreciate that. But I haven't heard a word from [Executive X] about it since. So Ray, my question to you is, do you really care about our input or not?

> **What was worse, *my* credibility was being questioned.**

Of course, I responded that I would look into it, that I do care about their input, and after the meeting I got on the phone with the guy I'm calling Executive X.

"What's going on?" I asked.

"Ray," he said, "we're working on it. We're going to get the answer and reply sometime next week."

"You don't understand," I said. "It doesn't matter what *your* schedule is. They want to hear from you. You could have at least sent back an answer, 'Great idea, we need to work through some things. We'll get back to you next week.' That would have been a response. But since he didn't hear a word out of you, your credibility is now being questioned." And what was worse, *my* credibility was being questioned.

If you're not going to respond to complaints or requests for support with a sense of urgency, you might as well not respond at all.

Hold Them Accountable

Once you've trained your people, answered their questions, and provided the support they need, you've got to take the next step, which is to hold them accountable. If you don't do that, the whole thing falls apart. I had this point driven home to me a couple of years after I came to Umpqua.

In those early years, we did everything we could think of to empower the frontline people to do whatever it took to improve the customer experience. "You don't need permission," we told them, "just go ahead and do it. Send them flowers, buy them candy, buy them dinner. Do whatever it takes." We thought we had done all the right things. We put money into a special account for each store to use for this purpose and we refilled it every quarter. We told them we wanted them to spend the money; it was safe to do so. We gave them examples of things that people had done to wow customers. We provided gift catalogs they could use, names of florists and candy stores. We supported them, in other words, and gave them the tools. I thought we had done the job and didn't think much more about it.

But after a while, three or four quarters, I realized I hadn't heard much about how this money was being used to delight our customers. So I asked Steve May for a report on how the money was being spent. Steve had the information compiled and brought the report to me.

"You're not going to like this," he said, shaking his head.

It turned out that some of the stores had several thousand dollars in their accounts. They weren't spending any of the money. This was very discouraging.

I had let things slide too long without checking back in, without holding people accountable. I learned that you've always got to follow up. One of the greatest mistakes leaders make is that they set standards and goals, but then don't go back and inspect and hold people accountable. Once you let accountability slide, you've basically neutered yourself. You've lost credibility. All you are doing is talking.

> I learned that you've always got to follow up.

So I told Steve to tell the managers of these stores to send the balances of their funds back and tell them that when we put more money in for the next quarter, we wanted it used as directed. If not, we'd take them out of the program and, if necessary, find new managers who would follow directions.

They got the message.

And that's the thing: *they didn't get the message until we inspected and followed up.* We put money into special accounts, we explicitly told them to spend it to delight customers, we gave them ideas about how to spend it, so you'd think it would be the easiest thing in the world to go ahead and spend it. How hard is it to spend money? But they didn't get the message until we followed up and asked, "Did you spend your money? If not, why not?"

Keep the Monkey Where It Belongs

I talked a lot earlier in this chapter about how important it is to support your people. And it is. But you have to do it in a way that keeps them accountable. You have to respond to their issues with a sense of urgency, as I said, but you have to do it in a way that keeps the monkey where it belongs, on their back. Let me give you an example.

At a focus group meeting about a year ago, Paul, a new store manager, told me he was having problems with his drive-up window. He had three lanes for drive-up and the machine in the third lane was constantly breaking down. Paul explained that his store was in a very busy location and two lanes couldn't handle the load. When one of the lanes was out of commission, the others would quickly turn into parking lots. This happened to be a store I drove by a lot and I knew Paul wasn't exaggerating. So I asked Paul if he had contacted our Facilities Department to come out and fix the third lane. He said he had and they were going to look into it, but that was a couple of weeks ago.

I said that was unacceptable. "Thank you for telling me that. Facilities will be in touch with you today. I promise you that."

So I paused, and he looked satisfied. But then I said, "Paul, what did *you* do about it?"

He looked at me with a puzzled expression. "Well, Ray, I'm not a mechanic. I don't know how to fix drive-up windows."

"I understand that. But you just told me how busy you are and how when one of the lanes backs up people get irritated at the congestion and long wait. So what I want to know is what did *you* do about it? What did you do to make that experience for our customers one of the best experiences they ever had with Umpqua Bank?"

He was befuddled. "What do you mean? I'm not sure I understand."

I said, "I'm not sure what I mean. But I'm sure you could have thought of something. If we're the world's greatest bank and something goes wrong, we take action. We think of ways to impress customers with how we respond when something goes wrong. We want our customers to go away talking about what we did to fix problems, not to go away taking about problems. And that's a huge difference.

"You could have had somebody out there handing out free soft drinks for the people who were stuck in line," I continued. "You could have told everybody how sorry we were for the delay and that we were going to put another ten bucks in their account. In the past, we've gone out and washed windshields. There are all kinds of things you could have done. You had the opportunity to sit down with your staff and talk about putting plans in place for things to do if anything went wrong anywhere in the bank. And you should have been ready for that if we're really serious about creating a one-of-a-kind customer experience."

Paul came to me for help and support that I was happy to provide. But I also turned around and held him accountable. You cannot pass the monkey to me. I'll help out, but it's still your monkey.

MOTIVATIONAL MOMENT

Ten Ways to Get Along Better
in This Great Big World

Gather participants together and read the following points.

- Before you say anything to anyone, ask yourself three things: Is it true? Is it kind? Is it necessary?
- Make promises sparingly and keep them faithfully.
- Never miss the opportunity to compliment or say something encouraging to someone.
- Refuse to talk negatively about others; don't gossip and don't listen to gossip.
- Have a forgiving view of people. Believe that most people are doing the best they can.
- Keep an open mind; discuss, but don't argue.
- Forget about counting to 10. Count to 1,000 before doing or saying anything that could make matters worse.
- Let your virtues speak for themselves.
- Cultivate your sense of humor; laughter is the shortest distance between two people.
- Do not seek so much to be consoled, as to console; do not seek so much to be understood, as to understand; do not seek so much to be loved, as to love.

Then ask others to contribute their own ideas for getting along better with others.

Chapter 7

Give Them the Power

While it's critically important to support your people and hold them accountable, that's not enough. You've also got to empower them by giving them permission to make decisions.

Why? It's simple. You've got no choice. We live in a real-time world. Things need to happen *now*. The only way to ensure that is to empower employees to make decisions on the spot, *right away*, to deal with issues as they arise. Don't make them run to you for permission.

In the past, the leader was the guy with the answers. Today, organizations have too many moving parts and business moves much too fast for people to run to leaders for answers. As a leader, you have to empower the people closest to the action to come up with *their own* answers.

No one else can do this for you. You've got to demonstrate it daily: you expect people to make decisions. Never even hint that people have to ask permission first. You have to make it clear that people will not be punished for making decisions, and especially won't be punished for good-faith mistakes.

Management experts have been pushing empowerment for years, so your eyes may be glazing over as you read this. But before you skip this chapter, ask yourself if you are genuinely satisfied that the people who work for you are contributing at 100 percent. Are you constantly bowled over by people at all levels of the company who seize the initiative, who see problems and just take care of them, who see opportunities and jump to take advantage of them? If so, great. But most executives I talk to feel that if they ever stop pushing, people will start backing off. If you feel that way, then you haven't really empowered your people.

What Empowerment Looks Like

A number of signs indicate whether or not people are empowered.

Empowered employees do not hesitate to tell the truth, good or bad.

I talk a lot in the first part of this book about how important it is for people to be able to tell the truth. It's the only way you can find out what is going on behind your back. But it's much more than that. People who aren't empowered to tell the truth aren't empowered to do much of anything. You can't tell somebody, "You are empowered, but be careful what you say."

You can send a message that tells people to watch what they say in an awful lot of ways. Sometimes just a cross look will do it. You've always got to be careful about sending an unintentional message that people should be careful about what they say. Awhile back, I took my executive team off site for a management retreat. During one session we got to talking about the good and the bad of my management style. One fellow, a recent addition to the executive team, decided to go after me. And not just me, he complained about our culture, our direction, and virtually everything about the company. And he wasn't being polite about it. Some of his language was pretty rude. Everybody in the room was looking at me, waiting for me to fire back. But I didn't.

> Everybody in the room was looking at me, waiting for me to fire back.

My blood was boiling, but I kept my cool. I knew that if I responded angrily, the meeting would be over. Everybody would shut down, and the whole retreat would be ruined. I had to stay focused on keeping people open and willing to contribute. Also, I thought, he might have been dumb to be so extreme, but it was also brave, being willing to take on the system and CEO. So after he finished his rant, I said, "That's interesting. Put that up on the board." If I had shut him down or been offended by his rude language, that would signal people to be careful about what they said. All my talk about empowerment would have been revealed as hollow. I never did confront him about it, even after the meeting. My feeling was that he had gone so far overboard that he embarrassed himself. But what was more important, I wanted people to feel absolutely safe in telling me whatever was on their minds. I still do.

Are people free to say what they think in your company?

When people are empowered, they get into a lot of debates, some very passionate.

A funny thing happens when people feel free to tell the truth. They start to disagree with each other and say so out loud. They all bring out their own points of view and put them on the table. They debate how to do things, what the customer really wants, marketing strategies, the direction the company should take, and so on. I encourage debate.

Whenever people in the bank have a disagreement about the company or what's best for the company, the ultimate winner in that debate is *always* going to be the company—as long as the leader or manager doesn't let it get personal. (When that happens, the debate becomes destructive.) But as long as a confrontation or disagreement is about the company, not about people, it's healthy. And I encourage it—maybe to the discomfort of some people who don't like open disagreements. I think it creates positive tension that encourages innovation.

Do you have lot of vigorous debates in your company? If not, your people are not empowered.

People who are empowered are not afraid of being punished for making decisions.

At Umpqua, people are never punished for trying to do something unique—what I call coloring outside the lines. What I will punish people for is not doing their jobs. But I tell our executives that nobody in this company should ever be criticized for trying to serve the customer. We might, however, recommend another way of handling the problem *next time*. "Thanks for taking care of the customer. If that comes up again, let me give you another idea to try that might work even better." That's different from criticism.

And you certainly don't punish or criticize someone for handling a situation differently from how you would handle it. One of our customers came into the bank very upset. She had accrued $700 in overdraft charges, an incredible amount. The Universal Associate she met with went over the charges with her and found they were all valid. It was the customer's fault for writing so many checks. But even so, the associate decided *on her own* to reverse almost all the charges, about $500. When the store manager found out about this, she was quite concerned. She didn't criticize the associate, because as I said, we never criticize people for trying to take care of customers. But she did ask why the associate would forgive $500 of charges. The associate explained that the customer was basically broke, and the bank would never collect the $700 anyway. But she wanted to impress upon the customer that the charges were her responsibility, so she didn't wipe them all away. When the associate explained her reasoning, it made sense. It was the right thing for the bank (since the bank was not going to collect that money anyway) and right for the customer.

Of course, at most companies, frontline associates would never be able to wipe out $500 in charges without permission. That sort of decision would be "above their pay grade." For most companies, especially in our industry, frontline people are not allowed to make many decisions. If there's a problem they've got to call a special number to get instructions because they are not allowed to deal with it. When people from other banks come to work for us, they say, "Wow, you guys get to handle these things on your own? People got fired for that where I used to work."

If you get frustrated that your people seem reluctant to make decisions, you need to look in the mirror and ask whether you've really made it safe for people to pull the trigger.

When people are empowered, they don't worry too much about the rules.

First of all, if you have a culture that really empowers people, you don't have a lot of rules to begin with. But even if you don't have a lot of overt rules, you'll find people often *look for* rules. "Have we ever done it that way before?" they'll ask, looking for permission from past practice. A lot of people are just not going to color outside the lines if they don't feel completely safe. They want rules because the rules give them security.

I like to tell my people not to be afraid to break rules.

Rules can't cover every eventuality. People shouldn't break rules just to break rules, but when it makes sense, they shouldn't let rules inhibit them from taking action. So I tell people, "Don't be afraid to break the rules, but

> I tell my people not to be afraid to break rules.

be prepared to explain why you did so. If you've got good reasons, people are going to pat you on the back and say 'way to go.' That's leadership, that's displaying initiative."

Some of the unwritten rules that people are wary of involve bureaucratic procedures. At one of our stores, the manager was concerned that the parking lot hadn't been striped in ten years. There were no lines at all, and it led to people parking at all sorts of angles and customer complaints. So our store manager followed procedures and put in a request with the Facilities Department to have the work done. When nothing happened she submitted another request and they said they'd get to it. Again, nothing happened. And customers were still complaining. Enough of that, the manager decided. She found some money in her budget, called a contractor, and had the parking lot stripes painted in.

Of course, not long after the paint job was completed, people from Facilities showed up. "This looks brand new," they said, "what's the matter?" The manager explained that she had hired a contractor and took care of it herself.

The people from Facilities got miffed because she didn't follow procedures and complained to her supervisor, Rick Carey, the head of retail. But Rick was pleased! "I think her initiative was wonderful," he told them. "If there is a problem here, it's with your responsibility to get things done as swiftly as we need." And he called the store manager and congratulated her for what she'd done.

If you defend bureaucratic procedures against individual initiative, you are sending the wrong message.

Set the Foul Lines

I talked a lot in the first part of the book about discipline and how important it is. It may seem strange now to be saying how important empowerment is. But I think they have to go together. People need to be empowered and they need to be disciplined. Without discipline empowerment turns into an "anything goes" culture. A lot of the people at Enron were empowered. But they weren't disciplined. And look where that got them.

Empowerment without discipline is a recipe for disaster.

Enforcing discipline while simultaneously encouraging initiative and empowerment is a tricky equation to manage and many companies struggle to get it right. My approach is to deal with it in terms of foul lines. As long as you keep the ball inside the foul lines, it's fair play. But once the ball goes outside the foul lines, you lose. You've got to set foul lines for your people: "Here is how far you can go, and if you do well with that, I might even let you go a little farther, but for now, here are the limits. Your job is to take care of the customer, and you can do it any way you want as long as you stay within these lines."

> When people don't know how far they can go, it scares the daylights out of them.

The point is that you are giving people direction and a goal, and allowing them to use their own ingenuity and creativity on how to reach it. You are not telling them what to do step by step, but you are setting bounds. You can do anything you want as long as you stay within the foul lines.

When people don't know how far they can go, it scares the daylights out of them. If I take you up in the mountains and put a blindfold on you and say go wherever you want, but don't go too far or you'll fall off the cliff, you won't move an inch because you don't know how far you can go. But if I tie a rope to your leg and say it's safe to go anywhere you want as long as the rope lets you, you'll feel free to move around.

When you set clear foul lines, people can feel safe in taking initiative and making decisions because they know how far they can go. So discipline and empowerment actually need to go together. For example, motivational moments are part of our discipline. If you are a manager of any sort of unit, you are required to have a motivational moment every morning. You are not empowered to decide you don't want to do motivational moments. But within that discipline, those foul lines, you are empowered to talk about *anything* you want.

On the front lines, we rely on our associates to take care of our customers and we empower them to do so as long as they stay within the foul lines. Let's say a client comes in and tells an associate that the bank down the street is paying 4 percent on CDs, but she's only getting 3.5 percent at Umpqua. She wants the associate to offer a better rate or she's going to move her business. The Umpqua associate has the ability to look at our relationship with that customer. If the customer's only connection with us is that CD account, we're going to pass. But if she has a checking account and other accounts with us, we want to keep that relationship, so we're going to try to match the interest rate of the bank down the street. And the associates are trained on making those decisions, and they are empowered to do so and congratulated for making those decisions.

But every now and then, we discover associates who are so intent on keeping a relationship that they'll renew those transactional accounts that have no other basic relationship with the bank. We've got to tell them that they've crossed a foul line.

Here is what we tell Umpqua associates about empowerment:

> Every Umpqua Associate has the freedom to identify a need, make a decision, and take action—wherever the need presents itself.
>
> With a shared vision that we must always take care of our customers and the community, there is nothing that stands in the way of an empowered Associate acting like a true neighbor to do what's right for a customer and the bank. Whether it's sending flowers to convey our thanks or coming up with a creative solution for a challenging loan, we each have the authority to "make the call" that guarantees an exceptional banking experience for our customers.
>
> And we mean it!

Celebrate and Reward Initiative

If you want people to take talk of empowerment seriously, you've got to show them you mean it. And that means you have to celebrate people who take initiative and reward them. At Umpqua, when an associate makes a decision to do what's right for a customer, we have programs in place that thank, reward, and recognize the associate—and that tell the story as an example for others to follow.

One of the ways we recognize associates who make a difference is the Brag Box, which is featured on Umpqua's internal Web site, called The Insider. Associates throughout the bank submit stories bragging about how coworkers made decisions to go above and beyond to solve customer problems or create extraordinary customer service. One recent brag recognized Kathy, a store manager who all on her own created a "Customer of the Month" program, which allowed all the associates in the store to take turns in selecting a customer for special appreciation. Another spotlighted an associate who had gone to extra lengths to help a customer who had fallen victim to one of those Nigerian fraud schemes. A basic theme of all the brags is that associates make decisions to do things, without asking permission.

Another program actually empowers associates to reward empowerment. I think of it as empowerment squared. Every team in the bank (a store or department) has a Team Recognition Fund, which is just a checking account that gets replenished every quarter with a specific amount of money based on the team's number of full-time equivalent employees. All associates have access to the fund to send something special (a gift certificate, flowers, dinner, or the like) to recognize another associate on the team or elsewhere in the bank. No permission or approval is required.

We have many other award programs—all designed to celebrate and reward people who are empowered to go above and beyond. I'll talk more about how we recognize and reward people in Chapter Twenty.

The Power of Empowerment

Nordstrom is well-known for its customer service. The employee handbook tells Nordstrom employees, "Use your own best judgment at all times." And they mean it. Let me share my own story.

I was in Tyson's Corner, Virginia, on business when I snagged a pair of dress slacks on something sharp. They were ruined. And that presented a problem, because I had to get on a plane later that day for another meeting in Boston and I didn't have another pair. There was a Nordstrom's across the street from my hotel, so I went over to the store and picked out a pair of slacks and took them to the counter with a completely unreasonable request: "I have a plane to catch and have to leave in three hours. Can you do the cuffs on these before I have to leave?"

The clerk was very apologetic and said he couldn't do that, but he could send them to my hotel in Boston by the next day. He was very sorry that he couldn't get it done in the unreasonable amount of time I was asking for, but assured me the pants would be at my hotel the next morning. So the next morning the box shows up at my hotel in Boston as promised. I opened it up and took my pants out, and then saw another pair in the box. And there was a note from the clerk in Tyson's Corner:

> Mr. Davis,
>
> I just want to say I felt bad about not being able to get your pants cuffed for you yesterday and putting you through the stress of worrying about whether they would arrive on time. I hope you will accept this second pair of pants as amends.
>
> Bill

Did that blow me away? Of course it did. Nordstrom has empowered its frontline people to make decisions to astound and delight their customers. Will I go back to Nordstrom's? You can count on it.

That's the power of empowerment.

MOTIVATIONAL MOMENT
Daily Survival Kit

Items Needed: Mint, candy Kiss, tea bag, eraser, rubber band, toothpick, gum, Band-Aid, pencil.

Exercise: Put all items in a self-sealing plastic sandwich bag. Make one package for each participant or pass one around the group. Ask each member to guess why the items in the bag can help you survive a day.

After everyone has guessed, read the following responses:

Toothpick: to remind you to pick out the good qualities in others.

Rubber band: to remind you to be flexible—things might not always go the way you want.

Band-Aid: to remind you to heal hurt feelings, yours or someone else's.

Pencil: to remind you to list the good things about your life.

Eraser: to remind you that everyone makes mistakes, and it's okay.

Gum: to remind you that when you stick with it, you can accomplish anything.

Mint: to remind you that you are worth a mint.

Candy Kiss: to remind you that everyone needs kindness every day.

Tea bag: to remind you to relax daily, reflect on the positive, and look forward to each new day.

Chapter 8

Rise Above the Battlefield

I get frustrated with my company if we're not creative enough, if we're not strategic enough. Occasionally, my executives get caught up in a battle, and even if they win it, they sometimes lose sight of the larger war. We can all fall into that trap. Leaders need to know what is happening on the front lines, but they also need to rise above the battlefield to achieve a strategic perspective on the company and where it is going.

We also need to be wary of falling into the trap of "this is the way we do things around here." No real leader would ever accept that as the justification for a practice or policy when it was spelled out in those words. But it's too easy to just accept the status quo either because you don't see alternatives or it's convenient. As a leader it's your job to bust paradigms and expose sacred cows—your own as much as other people's.

Here is what can happen when you don't rise above the battlefield. Wal-Mart has been a relentless growth machine—it's a company that knows how to grow and has learned how to manage that growth superbly. Its growth came in large part because it decided that it wasn't really in the retail business—at least as defined by its competitors—but in the supply chain business. It developed a superb logistics system that could track every penny of costs and it worked with suppliers to reduce costs and pass those savings on to its customers in the form of lower prices.

Wal-Mart executed that strategy superbly year after year, relentlessly. But while it was fighting its battle to squeeze out every penny of excess costs, it failed to rise above the battlefield to see what else was going on in the world. Its critics began to use Wal-Mart's very success in reducing costs as a way to attack it. Stories began appearing in the press alleging that the company used illegal immigrants, forced people to work off the clock, and paid so poorly that a large percentage of its workers had to rely on Medicaid. The company was slow to react to these allegations. It kept fighting its battle against costs without realizing the terrain had shifted. In early 2006 Maryland passed a law requiring Wal-Mart to increase its health care funding—and similar actions are planned in other states.

You don't have to agree with Wal-Mart's critics to realize that its executives were put on the defensive by these issues. It has public relations and political problems now that it didn't have before: problems it could have foreseen. It has been forced to play catch-up, when it might have been able to outflank its opponents if its executives had stopped a moment to rise above the battlefield.

> The history of business is littered with the bodies of companies that were superb at fighting battles.

The history of business is littered with the bodies of companies that were superb at fighting battles but lost their wars from lack of a broader view.

Several tools can help you get a view of the big picture—environmental scans, strategic planning retreats, and a veritable industry of consultants only too happy to prepare inch-thick reports for you. These tools can be valuable, but to my way of thinking, nothing can substitute for taking yourself out of the daily fray to gain perspective.

How to Gain Perspective

Here are some things I do to rise above the battlefield.

First of all, I take time to reflect. I just step off the train for a while and let it go on without me. My feeling is that Umpqua can get on just fine without me for a while. (If it can't, then I haven't been a very good leader.) When I leave the office, I really do leave the office. When I go on vacation, I tell people I'm not to be interrupted unless it's a real emergency. Getting out of the day-to-day rush allows me to think about things from a different perspective.

What does gaining perspective look like? It means stepping back and asking yourself questions like these:

- How have we changed in one, two, or three years?
- Where will we be in two, three, or five years? Is that where we really want to be?
- What aren't we paying attention to?
- What does our competition know that we don't?
- What is *really* going on here? (Apparent problems are often just symptoms of deeper issues.)

And you also need to step back and look at the big picture on a personal level, asking:

- Am I spending my time on the right things?
- Are my priorities in order?
- Do my activities match my priorities?
- Am I learning and growing enough to keep up as the company grows?
- Have I developed bad habits or blind spots that will hinder us going forward?
- Am I doing enough to help my executives rise above their own battlefields?

Leaders who for whatever reason fail to make time to ask these questions can end up being dragged along by events instead of charting their own course. Do you run from meeting to meeting? Is your desk so crammed with reports to read that it seems like you can never get ahead? Do you find yourself working harder and harder, thinking you are always playing catch-up? If so, you—and your company—are probably headed for a fall.

I also try to force myself out of my comfort zone. I try to snap my own rubber band. Most executives tend to favor their own strong suits, areas in which they have the most experience—finance, marketing, operations, human resources. If your background is in HR, you may tend to see everything through that lens and think every issue is, at heart, a people issue. If you're from operations, you might see everything as structural. My own background is in finance as well as sales and marketing, and believe me, I think marketing is tremendously important. But I know that I can't look at everything as a marketing issue. I've got to look at things from other perspectives as well, areas that don't come as naturally to me.

I try to read widely—in fact I stay away from publications that focus only on banks. I find I learn more from other kinds of businesses. I also make it a point to talk to executives from other industries, to see what's on their mind. Often what they are concerned with has nothing to do with us, but it can get me thinking differently. I ask myself, Is there a way that we can twist what they do so that it could work for us?

I also use our board of directors as a resource. I think too many CEOs just try to manage their board to get the board's approval for what they already want to do. I want to have a board that can help me, not rubber-stamp my plans. I think we have recruited outstanding people to serve on our board and I value their insights. They really do bring fresh perspectives and big-picture thinking. I'll talk more about our board in Chapter Thirteen.

Help Your People Rise Above the Battlefield

Your job as a leader of people is to help them rise above their own battlefields, to help them see the big picture. Too few managers can see beyond their own particular goals, so they can't focus on the bigger picture—where the company as a whole is headed.

As we've grown this company, the challenge has been to make sure my executives are marching at a much higher level than what is going on in the trenches. I don't want them looking down at the ground; I want their eyes to be on the horizon. I recently reorganized the whole corporation with this in mind. Let me tell you how it happened.

I was taking some time off and visiting Napa Valley, the wine region in California. I was sitting by the pool, enjoying the sun, and thinking about how I could prevent Umpqua from getting stuck fighting yesterday's war—only to look up to find that the war had moved onto a different battlefield. How could I get my people to think more strategically? My mind sort of wandered and I remembered an article I had read in *Fast Company* about a receptionist whose job title was Director of Smiles. It wasn't a very big piece, but it had made me think. By changing her job title, the company was saying that her job wasn't just to sit in the reception area and greet people.

Think about it. Her job was not only to smile at the customers and clients walking in, but to get them to smile. So her new job title really reflected what the company wanted her to do, her larger purpose.

So I started thinking about the job titles of my team at Umpqua. One of my key people, Lani Hayward, had the title of executive vice president of marketing. What is that about? It seemed pretty obvious: marketing, advertising, promotions, product development, customer research. If you have a generic title focus on marketing, that's all you're thinking about. How do my ads look? How are the promotions going? It's limiting.

So I asked myself, what do I *really* want this department to do? What's its larger purpose? And I thought, I've been telling Lani I want her to create strategies that will differentiate us in the marketplace. So why should I call her department the Marketing Department? Shouldn't it be called the Creative Strategies Division? And shouldn't Lani, the manager of the department, be called the EVP of creative strategies? If that is going to be Lani's job title, she is going to look at her job in a different way, on a higher level. Her job *just got bigger in her mind*, even though she's basically in charge of the same operations.

And then I thought about Barbara Baker, whose title was executive VP of human resources. Human resources—I turned that phrase over in my mind and I asked myself, *What the hell* is *human resources?* It sounded to me like you have a line of people with numbers stamped on their foreheads waiting for an assignment. If somebody needs to fill a position, HR reaches into a bag and grabs someone and says, "Here you go. Use this person." The whole picture was completely against what we are trying to do at Umpqua.

So I asked myself, what does our HR department really do? Train our associates through what we call the World's Greatest Bank University. Take care of benefits, records, and payroll. But the major focus of this division is to hire the right people, develop people in ways that fulfill them and help the company, and when necessary, move the right people out. And what that meant to me was that the group's real job in the company was to enhance the culture of the company. Culture is all about people: people enhance our culture and the culture sustains our people. So I changed the name of the group to the Cultural Enhancement Division. If you're the director of HR, you're worried about how

> The whole picture was completely against what we are trying to do at Umpqua.

much this guy gets paid, have we filed the benefits paperwork right, those types of operational issues. But if you're in charge of cultural enhancement, you're going to start thinking at a much higher level.

I also reorganized and renamed all the other departments in the company. The IT Department is now the Technology Advancement Department because I want them to *advance* the technology in my company. I don't want them to maintain it or keep it the same. Finance is now Financial Integrity, because their responsibility is to keep the integrity of our financial statements top drawer, never questionable.

The impact this has had on my execs has been profound. It has forced them to get out of the trenches, get off the battlefield and up on higher ground. It has helped them stop thinking of things in operational terms and start thinking in more strategic terms.

Like "director of smiles," "EVP of cultural enhancement" or "creative strategies" may sound corny, but I think simple things work well. Lots of things we do might sound silly to others, like saying we're "The World's Greatest Bank." By now you know it's not silly to us; it's our state of mind, what we strive to become.

But think about that a minute: as a leader, do you have anything more important to do for the people you lead than ensure that their state of mind stays focused on the important goals of the company?

You can't influence their abilities. You can't influence the work experience they came on board with. But you *can* influence their state of mind.

If you as a leader can influence your people's state of mind effectively, you've taken a big step toward your goals. Changing job titles sounds like just changing words on paper, but at Umpqua it has changed the way people think about their jobs. It's taken the mind-set and moved it up a level.

Another way to help your managers gain perspective and see the big picture is to encourage them to teach. When you have to explain your job and areas of responsibility to someone else, it makes you think about them in a different way. A while ago, we created a "Student Board of Directors" program to give outstanding high school students an opportunity to learn about banking, work at the bank if they wished, get some financial assistance with college, and conduct a community project. It was started as a community relations initiative, but it turned out that the benefits to the officers of the bank were equally important. Officers and managers from the bank made presentations on their particular areas of expertise to the student board at their monthly board of directors meetings, and just doing that got them thinking about their jobs in a new way.

Teaching gives you the opportunity to step back and take a fresh look at your job. As you organize your thoughts you may discover things you never articulated before. You might think to yourself, Holy smoke, why am I doing that? It also gets you to focus. If you're going to talk about a topic, it makes you get up to speed on it. Almost all our executives and managers teach regularly at our training and development unit, the World's Greatest Bank University. It's expected of them, not just because they have an obligation to help their associates learn, but also because it's important in their own development. It helps them step back and get a view of the operation they're running from a higher plane.

> A leader's job
> is to bust
> paradigms
> and expose
> sacred cows.

Busting Paradigms

As I said at the beginning of this chapter, a leader's job is to bust paradigms and expose sacred cows—your own and your people's. I think paradigm busting is critically important in everything we do. We've always got to ask, Why are we doing it this way? Helping people look at things from a higher perspective enables them to see possibilities and alternatives they may have overlooked. This is especially important when your company is growing at a rapid clip. People can be so immersed in just keeping up with all the changes growth brings that they lose sight of the goal line. You need to help them step back so that they can take charge of the changes and not be dragged along by them.

MOTIVATIONAL MOMENT
The Human Spider Web

Solving this exercise depends on someone's capacity to see the whole picture, assume a leadership role, and communicate clearly. It works best with a small team.

Exercise: If you have a large team, divide it into groups of six to eight individuals. Have each group move to a location that allows the members to stand in a small circle. Instruct members of each group to extend their hands across the circle and grasp the hands of the other members who are approximately opposite them—left hand to right, with everyone holding hands with *two* different people. Then inform them that their task is to unravel the spider web of the interlocking arms without letting go of anyone's hands.

   If you have one team, inform them that they will be timed (as a way to place pressure on them); if you have several groups, tell them they will be competing with other groups to see who finishes the task first.

Discussion: Ask people to talk about the following questions:

- What was your first thought when you heard the nature of the task? (Probably "This will be impossible!")
- What member behaviors detracted (or could detract) from the group's success in achieving its goal?
- What lessons does this exercise have for future team building?

Tip: The key lies in having participants step over one another's arms to disentangle themselves until a circle is complete. Therefore, it is recommended that all team members be wearing suitable (that is, casual, easy to move in) clothes.

Chapter 9

Explain Your Movie

When I came to Umpqua, as I've said, I told people I had a motion picture running in my head about the future of the company: what I wanted to create. But I also told them I couldn't project it on a screen for them to see. All I could do was attempt to articulate it to make it real for them. However, they had to understand that something is always lost in translation.

That's the thing about visions. They are always a little hazy; a motion picture playing in your head never has all the details filled in. And that's okay. In fact, that's the way it should be.

Visions are not goals. Goals are statements like, "We will become number 1 in market share within three years." They are cut-and-dried and pretty much explain their own meaning. But vision statements have to be a bit nebulous. Unlike a goal, which you meet or not, a vision is always out there, pointing the way to the future. It creates a positive tension that gives you something to keep striving for. The movie playing in my head always gets a little better. It seems to be a never-ending story.

Visions are important because they help motivate people, they get people rowing in the same direction, and they help people make good decisions.

Our vision is to be the world's greatest bank. But what does that mean? Does it mean the world's biggest, or most profitable, or fastest growing, or . . . what? In fact, it doesn't mean any of those things. The thing about most vision statements, ours included, is that they are short on details. They don't explain their own meaning.

That's your job as a leader.

Leaders who don't make it a top priority to help people see the vision of the company are making a big mistake. Instead of talking about the vision and making it real, they focus on this month's numbers or next quarter's numbers. I know numbers are important—and everybody at Umpqua knows it too—but they're important *because they help us fulfill our vision.* If we are financially healthy, then we have the wherewithal to advance our vision. But make no mistake, our quest is for the vision, not the numbers. If all you talk about is the numbers, people will lose sight of the vision.

> The numbers are important because they help us fulfill our vision.

And if you think having a vision is just a tool for rallying the troops and whipping up enthusiasm so that they'll make the numbers, sooner or later, you'll end up with no vision *and* weak numbers. A lot of companies—AT&T, Sears, Kmart, General Motors, Compaq, a whole long, sad list—aren't what they used to be because after years of growth they lost track of what they were really trying to do.

From Vision to Action

When we say we aim to be the world's greatest bank, it's more than an expression, more than a slogan. It's our commitment to our customers and communities, and, as I've said, *it's our commitment to ourselves.* It's the reason for everything we do. For us being the world's greatest bank means a number of things. And what it meant in 1996 isn't exactly what it means today and probably won't be exactly what it means five years from now. Some of the things it means:

- We go beyond outstanding customer service to surprise and delight our customers.
- We are so distinctive that when you walk into one of our stores you know right away not only that you are in a bank but that you're in an Umpqua bank.
- We are an outstanding place to work.

- We are a responsible corporate citizen in every community we serve.
- We maintain the highest standards of financial integrity.
- We provide our shareholders with an excellent return on their investment in us.
- We live our values every day.

You won't find these bullet points in any Umpqua document. They're not part of our official vision at all. Our vision is living and breathing, growing and evolving—just as our company is. You can't nail it down with words on a piece of paper. The way to articulate your vision is not to spell out the details—but to translate it into action every single day.

Now I am not saying you shouldn't go out and give speeches about your vision for the company. Far from it. You can't come up with a vision and have it sit on your desk. You've got to be out talking about it all the time. But if all you do is give speeches, you won't get very far. It's much more important to bring your vision to life with *action*.

You've got to be out and about translating vision into action by word and deed. The simple truth is that you have to live your vision every day—and you have to do it visibly. When you're a leader, people watch every move you make. They want to know if you are serious about your vision for the company. If you aren't out making sure that you're advancing the vision of the company every day, then your people won't be either.

But if you are serious about your vision and people can see that in what you say and do and in how you spend your time, then you have a chance to get your movie playing in their minds. I take the view that if I can get others in the company to view the same motion picture, or inspire others to have their own piece of the picture that's congruent, then we're going to win. Nobody will be able to touch us.

When you have communicated a clear vision for your company, you've taken a big step to help people rise above the battlefield, as I discussed in Chapter Eight. When people understand the vision for the company, they can see more clearly how all the pieces fit together. They can make their own decisions to turn the vision into reality and not wait for management. They don't have to wait for

you to tell them what to do next. It creates a sense of empowerment that generates energy, commitment, and passion.

I've mentioned the focus group meetings I have with frontline
associates and the Town Hall meetings we have every quarter. I
think these are vital tools for supporting our people, but they are
more than that. They help me demonstrate what our vision of
being the world's greatest bank means in concrete detail. In Chapter Six, the story of Paul, the store manager who had a drive-up
window that was breaking down and complained that the Facilities
Department was slow to repair it, illustrates this point. I promised
that facilities would contact him that same day, and then turned
around and held him accountable for making sure that customers
came away thinking about what we did in response to the problem
rather than how inconvenient that problem was. In that exchange,
I demonstrated what one aspect of being the world's greatest bank
really means.

Keep Your Vision Fresh

Earlier I mentioned some companies like Sears and Compaq that
lost track of what they were really trying to do over years of
growth. They didn't keep their vision fresh and relevant. If you
are growing your company, that can become a problem. As you
get bigger and bigger, it's natural to focus on keeping up with
your own growing pains and take your eye off of where you are
headed. If you focus just on growth in revenue, assets, or market
share, you become complacent and lull yourself into thinking that
your growth means everything is clicking. That's dangerous.
Growth presents challenges to your vision that you have to keep
an eye out for.

The test we now face, since growing to more than $7 billion in
assets and 128 locations, is whether we can keep the focus on our
vision as intense and razor-sharp as it was back in 1996, when we
were just starting our revolution. I worry that our growth will produce bureaucratic creep that will cloud our vision for the company.
Some of the things I look for include these warning signs:

- People are serving the infrastructure more than the customer.
- Local decisions are being run up to headquarters.

- Talk about numbers limits discussions about vision, mission, and values.
- Rules and policies keep multiplying.
- Customers with problems get batted around from department to department.

I watch for these symptoms of bureaucratic creep like a hawk. To ward them off, you've got to keep your vision fresh, and you also need to manage your culture actively, which I discuss in Part Five.

What are the things you worry about that might get in the way of your vision? They're out there, I promise you. Don't let them sneak up on you. Be alert for the warning signs before troubles start creeping up.

Keep Your Vision Clean

As we've grown, I've come to see ever more clearly that our challenge is to remain a community bank. When we were smaller, it sort of went without saying: of course we were a community bank. We served the small communities where we were located, taking in local deposits and investing in local businesses. It wasn't important to emphasize our business model as a community bank when we had a dozen stores, mostly in smaller Oregon towns. Now that we have well over a hundred stores all over Oregon, southern Washington, and northern California, we can't take it for granted anymore that *of course* we're a community bank.

I have had to emphasize this more and more as I talk about our vision for the company. Yes, we're growing. Yes, we're acquiring other banks, but we are committed to remaining a community bank. People in our industry say if you're big you can't be a community bank. That's not true. It has nothing to do with size: it's about the way you operate the business, the culture you maintain, the relationships you build, and the way you serve customers.

But you run a particular risk when you use mergers and acquisitions as one of your tools for growth. People can start thinking that your strategy is simply acquisitions and that your vision for the company is all about size. Don't let that perception gain ground. Stamp it out or it will weaken your vision and your prospects.

> People can start thinking that your strategy is all about size. Don't let that perception gain ground. Stamp it out!

We tend to make a major acquisition every few years. This practice is a continual source of criticism. A lot of people think we're acquisitions junkies and that's our whole strategy. They'll ask me, "Ray, how many people do you have on your M&A team who are out talking to people, talking deals." I tell them I don't have an M&A team. That's not our style. Sure, if someone thinks a deal might work for us, I'll give them a call. But we don't have people out making calls, scouting for deals, the way the big banks do. It's not our core strategy and it's not part of our vision. I continue to stay focused on our original vision and our strategy of differentiating ourselves from the competition to produce organic growth.

We wouldn't have to put the huge focus on customer service, marketing, design, and creating a unique customer experience in our stores if our strategy was to grow by acquisitions. Nor would we go to the expense of rebranding acquired banks and training the new people in our unique way of doing business. Acquisitions were not part of our original strategy, which focused on knowing what business we were really in, as I described in Chapter One. But now what has happened is that we have developed such a strong reputation as a company that is able to complete transactions and successfully integrate acquired companies—operationally, culturally, and the like—that we've become what banks call "an acquirer of choice." Because so much has been written about us, from time to time other companies come to us and ask to get on the Umpqua train. They think it would make sense to partner with us. If you're going to sell your bank, we're one of the two or three banks you'll call.

So now acquisitions have become an adjunct to our core growth strategy and a means to fulfilling our vision. But any acquisition has to meet two criteria. The first is the strategic rationale: Why would we buy that bank? The answer can't be just to make us bigger. That's not our motivation. Strategically, how does it advance our brand? How does it help our footprint? How does it help move us on the road to being The World's Great Bank? And can it get us there faster than if we opened our own stores one at a time? The second, of course, involves the financial metrics. Can we make it a good deal for our shareholders? When the opportunity comes along to make an acquisition that fits our criteria, we do.

But I don't let our success with acquisitions obscure our vision for the company, which remains the same, to be "The World's Greatest Bank." That's the motion picture that keeps playing in my head.

 MOTIVATIONAL MOMENT

The Power of Communication

Exercise: Purchase small Lego kits (space ship, monster, and so on—the more unusual the better) and keep them hidden until the participants have formed teams of three. Place two of the team members back to back, one with the pieces and the other with the instructions, while the third person observes. Direct the person with the pieces to build the item following oral instructions from the one with the directions. After several minutes, the observer and instructor can switch roles.

Conclusion: Assembling a kit in this fashion is a lot of fun and a very powerful demonstration of how important communication is to success as a team.

Chapter 10

Be Real

If you can't be yourself, you can't lead. It's as simple as that.

When you're leading a company—especially if you're new to the company as I was—everyone watches you like a hawk. *Like a hawk.* Everything you say and do will be noted and analyzed six ways from Sunday. *Everything.* This was driven home to me as I was preparing to write this book.

I was asking around for stories from the early days, trying to refresh my memory, and I got this story from Sandy Hunt, who was then my assistant and is now VP for culture. It's about one of my first "get to know you" visits to an Umpqua store for an informal meeting with associates over pizza. According to one of the associates Sandy spoke to (I'll call her Meg), we were talking and the subject turned to me and where I came from. When I said I had been living most recently in Atlanta, Meg asked about the Braves baseball team and said she was a big fan. So, according to what Meg told Sandy, we talked about the Braves for a minute, and then I cut it off with the comment, "I'm not here to talk about baseball."

Meg told Sandy she thought I was cold.

Now, personally I don't remember the details of this long-ago meeting. Did I cut her off? Maybe. But that's not the point. The kicker is this added detail from Sandy. "This happened almost twelve years ago, and the associate remembers it *like it was yesterday.*"

You have an impact on people whether you like it or not. They watch every move you make. They watch so closely that if there's anything phony or fake, they'll spot it. You have got to be yourself.

(Meg, by the way, is still with the company. She's a store manager now. She's still a Braves fan, and she's become a big fan of our Umpqua culture.)

Leading is hard work. It can be exhausting. And you can't do it well while you're pretending to be someone else. So if you're not comfortable in your own skin, you're going to have a hard time leading people. That isn't to say you might not do pretty well using carrots and sticks to get people to go along. But that's not *leading* in my book.

> If you're not comfortable in your own skin, you're going to have a hard time leading people.

Bring Your Personality to Work

Every company assumes the personality of the leader. If you are a little bit nutty, the company is going to take on that nuttier approach. If you were to ask my executives about me, they'd say, "I think Ray is hard to predict." They've told me that many times. They don't know what I'm going to do next.

Being unpredictable goes against the conventional wisdom from Management 101 that says you should be level, be stable, so people know where they stand and can get on with doing their jobs. Well, I'm not so focused on that. I want to *inspire* people. I don't want people to keep their heads down, like they're producing widgets on an assembly line. I want them fired up! I want them to step out, take risks, and move this company forward. So I'm not going to be mild-mannered and predictable. Maybe I'm wrong, but that's the way I am and that's the way I do it. Some things, I do wish I was more predictable about. But in other areas I refuse to be predictable, because I like people to be on their toes.

My company runs fast. We make decisions and we move. I like it that way, that's my style. I think a sense of urgency is important.

If you have a sense of urgency, you can't manage by memos and e-mail. A sense of urgency gets bogged down by e-mail. If you want to slow things down, send e-mail. I've seen more hamster wheels spinning over e-mail than any other communications mode.

If you want to get something done, *pick up the phone and talk it through*. Instead of picking up a phone for a two-minute phone call that gets something done, people will spend ten minutes typing up e-mail, which has to be responded to, which then has to be responded to, and so on and on.

I like to get up close and personal. As I've said, you can't lead by remote control. I make myself accessible. I suppose the other side of this is that I'm not a big believer in the concept of chain of command, which I am sure some management experts would also criticize me for. I don't intentionally bypass the chain of command, but people know the culture of this company comes from me. I'm the father of it. It's my responsibility. And people need to hear from *me*.

So I believe in dealing directly with people, whether it's a senior VP at headquarters, a store manager in California, or a frontline associate. Sure, you can go through the chain of command, talk to the senior VP, who talks to the VP, who talks to the assistant VP, who talks to the regional manager, and then finally to the person affected—and in three days if you're lucky, but more likely three weeks, you'll get some results. We live in a real-time world, though, and that just doesn't cut it. If something is bothering someone, if there is a problem or an opportunity, you need to deal with it *now*.

> If there is a problem or an opportunity, you need to deal with it *now*.

Now is a great word—and *I'll get around to it* is the kiss of death.

I have a sense of urgency and my staff know it! They joke that all my priorities are number 1. That's not really true, but I'm sure it seems that way sometimes. I expect our executives to have the same sense of urgency that I have, especially when it comes to supporting our frontline people. When that breaks down, I get pretty upset with them. No question about it. If there's anything you're doing to help customers, or your employees and associates, or a project that will improve the company in some way—whether it will make a big difference or a little difference, then do it, just do it, right now! Just go ahead and do it right away!

Call any of the executives in this company and they'll have a story to tell you about how I came after them like a heat-seeking missile over some problem. Failure to act urgently on a customer's problem is a take-away from our culture and I'm not going to tolerate it. I mean business on this. I'm relentless, I won't let up.

If I get a letter or e-mail and a customer is having some sort of problem, I'll turn it over to the EVP of retail (if he's the appropriate guy) and ask him to take care of it right away. And I'll keep a copy of the original, so I can follow up. I tell him to let me know when he's taken care of it so I can take it off *my* to-do list. And if I see him later in the day, I'll ask if he's handled it. And if he hasn't yet, I'll say, "I want it done before you leave *today*." These people are waiting for a response. To us it may seem like small potatoes and we'll get around to it next week. Bull! To the customer it's a big problem.

I have extremely high standards for our executive team. And sometimes I push too hard on people and they push right back. But that's okay. I can take it. Awhile ago, I got to riding one of my top people for a mistake I thought had been made.

I guess I touched a sore spot once too often. This person whirled around on me.

"What do you want from me, Ray? You want me to say I screwed up? Okay, I screwed up! Now knock it off!"

If you've got strong people working for you, you've got to expect some give-and-take. If you don't have people pushing back on you once in a while, you've really got to question yourself. Are you just hiring yes-men? Do you just want to hog the stage? Do you just want to be liked?

Although I can be hard on my team, I am also loyal to them. I will give them the benefit of the doubt every single time. But if you are just skating along and wasting people's time, you have a problem. I'm not going to mess with you. I'm loyal to people who are singing our song.

I'm not concerned about being liked. What's more important to me is that people like Umpqua, and like working here. That's what I worry about.

Let Your Hair Down

One other thing: you've got to let your hair down. Let your people see you not just in a business environment but also in a social environment, where you're not "Mr. CEO" or "Ms. CEO." We used to have company picnics when we were smaller. (Unfortunately, it's not practical now that we are so geographically dispersed.) I cooked the hamburgers. I'd be there in my Levi's, flipping burgers, burning some, dropping some, joking and laughing with people. It was fun.

So don't walk around with your CEO badge on all the time. People need to know you're human and that you don't mind flipping hamburgers, visiting with their kids, sitting down with their families, and making friends. They need to see you having fun. People have to know it's okay to have a good time.

A new associate once came up to me and said, "You know, Ray, at my previous bank, we could never laugh. A supervisor would give us a look that said, 'Get back to work.' But here, we laugh our heads off at things, and our customers come in and want to know what we're laughing at. They want to be let in on the joke and they appreciate we're having so much fun at work. It's so positive."

I said, "Well, keep laughing. I want you to have fun." I like to laugh. Doesn't everyone? I believe work should be fun. Winning the race is fun. Beating the competition is fun. And people should be able to enjoy it.

Show Your Feelings

I admit, sometimes I get a little emotional. I'll never forget one experience when we were designing our next-generation store—the one in Portland's Pearl District that I described earlier. I was walking by Ziba, the design firm we hired, and I decided to go in unannounced to see how they were progressing. I couldn't believe what I saw. The room looked like that scene in the movie *A Beautiful Mind,* where Nash has papers with formulas plastered over every square inch of space. Every square inch of wall was covered with something. Design ideas for our new store were everywhere. There were six young people huddled together, discussing something so intently that they didn't notice me come in. I coughed a little, and one of them looked up. "Oh, hi, Ray. Sit down and join us."

I looked around a moment, and said, "I'm sorry, I can't. I'll see you guys later, I just wanted to stop by and say hello." And as I walked out, I had the most wonderful, warm feeling in my gut. Here were six young people working away trying to make our company better. The creative juices flowing in that room were palpable. I had to get out of there so I wouldn't break the spell. I never felt so good about the company. These young people were figuring out how to interpret that moving picture that's always playing in my head.

Leaders who really care about what they are building are going to have strong feelings about it. When you see your people all pulling together for the good of the company, it should make you proud and give you that warm feeling in your gut. When people respond to your vision and work to take it to the next level, it should fill you with gratitude and appreciation. And on the other hand, when people get distracted from the vision or put their own concerns ahead of the company's, you'll naturally get a little riled up. I don't think you should hide those feelings from your people. It's good to show people your pride, gratitude, and appreciation—and when appropriate, your concern, displeasure, and impatience.

I think leaders who bottle up all their emotions are making a mistake. If you don't show your feelings, people will think you're aloof and detached. You don't want to be inscrutable. If they don't know what you are feeling, they'll tend to be more wary. In short, if you are not open with them, they won't be open with you. And one more thing: when you do try to show your enthusiasm at a company meeting or similar situation, they'll think it is all an act.

> Most of the people you work with closely already see your weaknesses—probably more clearly than you do.

Believe me, my people know it when I'm jazzed and when I'm displeased. I don't keep things a secret. I don't try to be anything but who I am. I am not a complicated guy. I don't pretend to be sophisticated. I don't think leading a company is rocket science.

What this all comes down to is that you've got to be able to express your personality at work. If you always have your guard up, you just won't be as effective as a leader. Some leaders keep people at a distance because they are unsure of themselves and don't want their weaknesses exposed.

Well, I've got news for you. Most of the people you work with closely already see your weaknesses—probably more clearly than you do. And keeping people at a distance will only make you look weak and lacking in confidence. Sure, you take some risks exposing yourself, but there is really no alternative. Nobody is going to be led by a robot.

There is a flip side to this. You've got to let your people be real too. Let them be themselves. Let them bring their whole personalities to work. Then they can bring all their enthusiasm, inspiration, and energy to work too.

 MOTIVATIONAL MOMENT

Getting to Know You

Exercise: Have each participant write down something personal—something about their family, their childhood, their hobbies, and so on. It should be something they haven't shared with anyone else in the group. Gather the responses and read each one out loud, while the group tries to guess who it belongs to.

This generates some interesting and enjoyable discussion about the team.

Part Three

Master the Basics

A football team doesn't get to the Super Bowl just because it's got a great quarterback. Any team that reaches the Super Bowl has to be very good at blocking and tackling, which enables the quarterback to shine. In other words, you have to be good at the basics before you step out and do the unusual. A company can have a CEO who's really talented, but if the organizational infrastructure isn't strong enough to support that talent, the company is going to struggle. On the other hand, when the core is solid, you are in a better position to take risks. If you do throw a long pass that's incomplete, it's not the end of the world. You can regroup and try again, because you've got a solid foundation.

There is no rocket science in this section of the book, just commonsense basics—but too often these basics get short shrift. You cannot transform your company if you aren't very good at getting the basics right.

Sweat the small stuff. I don't care how great your strategy is, if you can't make it work flawlessly on the ground, you're not going anywhere. And you can't execute your strategy if you don't sweat the small stuff.

Pick the right people. In *Good to Great,* Jim Collins says that you've got to get the right people on the bus. I think that is exactly right. But who are the right people? It's not about job skills, it's about attitude—that sparkle in the eye that says "I'm ready for anything." When people have that attitude, your company is ready to take the journey of continuous transformation.

Develop your board. Companies can't grow if they are unable to move fast. And they can't move fast if the executive team has to drag the board of directors along with it. I describe how I work with my board to keep us all aligned and on track.

Don't overlook the intangibles. In a competitive environment in which products and services are almost always interchangeable, you cannot grow your company without paying close attention to the intangibles.

Chapter 11

Sweat the Small Stuff

I have a disease.

If I walk into a store and something is out of place or doesn't look right, I spot it. If there is something worn or broken, I'll see it. If a lightbulb is burned out, I'll notice it. I don't look for these things, but somehow they just jump out at me. That's why I call it a disease.

I go on the road to visit our facilities regularly. These are not surprise visits. I always call ahead and let them know I'm coming—I don't think it is fair to surprise people and play "gotcha" with them. But no matter how hard they work to spruce things up, if something isn't quite right, I'll see it. And after I point it out, you should see the look on their faces. "How did he see that? We've been looking at that for a year, and we never noticed it."

I recently went into a newly acquired store in California, which had just put up our Umpqua signage. I noticed that there seemed to be something wrong with our logo sign. I stared at it a while, and it finally hit me: it was backwards. Our logo has a pine tree and it curves ever so slightly to the right. Putting it up backwards made a subtle difference—see Figure 11.1. It wasn't obvious, but it caught my eye. As I said, I have this disease.

It had been up there for all to see for weeks! The sad thing is that the store manager hadn't noticed it. The kicker came when one of the associates told me, "You know, a couple of customers mentioned it to us." So I had to take the manager aside and talk to her about the importance of details.

FIGURE 11.1   THE UMPQUA LOGO, RIGHT AND WRONG

I notice the details because I care about them. I don't call people out over these details because I'm playing gotcha or trying to put people down—I do it to say to people, *please have a sense of pride in this company and what we stand for.* I do it to let people know that anything that affects the customer experience is important.

The thing is, the small stuff makes a big difference to your customers and to your business.

Richard Carlson has a popular book called *Don't Sweat the Small Stuff—and It's All Small Stuff,* where he advises people not to get worked up when someone cuts in front of you in line, or when a clerk is rude to you in a store. His point is that you shouldn't allow yourself to be provoked by such slights as it's a waste of energy. And on a personal level, I suppose he's right. You shouldn't stew all day long if a clerk is rude to you. On the other hand, if it's your store and that clerk is being rude to one of your customers, it is a very big deal. *In business, you've got to sweat the small stuff.*

When people deal with a reputable company, they expect the large things to be done right. At a bank, you expect your checking accounts to be handled correctly and the interest on your savings account to be computed accurately. When you go to a tire store, you expect the tires to be mounted on your wheels and balanced properly. It's taken for granted. What you don't expect are the little things. And what you remember is not how well the tires were balanced but whether the guy behind the counter went out of his way to help you or was rude to you or whether the coffee tasted like it had been sitting there for days. It's the things that happen that you don't expect that either delight or irritate you. It's all in the details. Sweat the details.

> If the small things are important to the executives, I promise they are going to be important to the frontline people.

I sometimes ask our customers to "tell me the biggest thing Umpqua has done for you," and they stumble around trying to find an answer. But if I ask them to tell me one of the smallest things, they usually come up with an answer quickly, something like, "Oh, Sarah the teller sent us cookies the other day." That's what people remember and that's what they talk about.

Too many times, leaders take the small stuff for granted. And it goes back to accountability. If the small things are important to the executives, I promise they are going to be important to the frontline people. I believe that the companies that are great, that excel, that stand out, that have reputations for excellence in any area are the ones that pay attention to detail. More than that, they have a sense of urgency in getting the details right.

Protecting Your Brand

Attention to detail isn't just about customer service: it's critical to your brand. Your brand depends on everything you do, how you present yourself, how you treat people, how you stand behind your products or services. You can't have a strong brand and be lax about the details.

Disney, for example, has one of the premiere brands in the world. Walt Disney was a master at paying attention to detail and his company still operates that way today. I once talked to Mike Vance, who was in charge of idea and people development for Walt Disney Productions, Disneyland, and Walt Disney World. He was also dean of Disney University, famed for its training programs.

Mike told me about the incredible attention to detail that Disney achieved in managing the huge crowds it has to deal with. For example, he told me that Walt Disney World has a system for people who can't remember where they parked in the huge lots: if you can remember when you arrived, they'll take you to the row where you left your car. If you left your car running—some people are actually in such a rush to get into the park they leave the car running—they have a way to get into your car and turn it off. The parking attendants all carry radios, but they're always on the left side, because they don't want people to think they're guns.

When people go to the ticket counter, the music they hear is by John Philip Souza—marching music to get people moving on into the park. Inside the park, although the stands sell a lot of popcorn and candy, you never see a piece of popcorn or a candy wrapper on the ground—people work constantly to sweep up litter. Disney sweats the details—and the results speak for themselves.

If management can push that sort of training and attention to detail down to the front lines so consistently, to me it speaks volumes about the quality of the company and its management team. Few companies are like Disney, and if you run across one, get to know it well. You can learn a great deal from such companies.

It's about standards and having the will to maintain them. And it starts with the details. If you can't get the details right, why should your customers expect you to get the big things right?

The physical appearance of our Umpqua stores is a major part of our brand, and that's why I seem to have that disease I mentioned earlier. But it's more than making sure that everything is in good condition.

As I've said, a major part of our strategy is not to look like other banks, and in fact to operate our facilities as stores. When we were designing our first concept store in Roseburg—the one I described in Chapter One—the question came up of whether we should decorate the store with plants. Plants are a common decoration in banks. But retail stores are full of things for sale and a great deal of effort is spent displaying the products attractively. They don't have plants. So I said no to the idea of plants and when the store opened there were no plants anywhere. But then something happened.

I went into the store one day and saw plants everywhere. I asked Neal Brown, the store manager, where the plants had come from. He said a VP had gotten them from The Plant Lady, one of those companies that take care of plants in office buildings. So I called this VP and asked why he put plants in the store. He said he just thought he'd warm it up a little bit.

> "That's not a problem. Tell them the plants will all be in the parking lot."

So I said, "Here's what I want done. Please call The Plant Lady and tell them to get the plants out of there."

"But Ray, we have a three-month contract on these plants."

"I don't care what we've got," I replied. "I want all those plants out of the bank by noon today."

"Well, that's pretty short notice. They probably can't get over here till later in the afternoon."

I said, "That's not a problem. Tell them the plants will all be in the parking lot." Needless to say, the company got there before noon and took the plants away. You can't protect your brand by being sloppy about the details.

Do Things Well

I don't care how great your strategy is, if you can't translate it down to make it work flawlessly on the ground, you're not going anywhere. You can't execute your strategy if you don't sweat the small stuff.

Leaders who think paying attention to execution at the finest level is too much work or who think they can delegate it to someone else are doomed to mediocrity. Listen to Larry Bossidy, who was chairman and CEO of AlliedSignal and then chairman of Honeywell International after it acquired AlliedSignal. He wrote a best-selling book titled *Execution: The Discipline of Getting Things Done* and later described his main points in *Leader to Leader,* a journal for and largely by top executives. He faults top leaders who see execution as tactics, seeing that side of business as something that can be delegated while the leadership focuses on so-called bigger issues. As he points out, "Getting things done isn't 'tactics,' it's the heart and soul of a company. Execution is everything. It produces satisfied customers and repeat business, higher operating margins

Getting things done is the heart and soul of a company.

and earnings per share. Leaders who do not pay attention to how their companies get things done are running companies that don't do things well." He adds that excellent execution requires constant attention: "You are always executing as compared to your competitor. If you don't continue to get better you will be getting worse."

I agree with Bossidy. How you do the small stuff is the heart and soul of your company. Do you want to run a company that doesn't do things well? I thought not. You've got to sweat the small stuff.

 MOTIVATIONAL MOMENT

First Impressions

Exercise:
- Give each participant a piece of paper and a pencil with an eraser.
- Ask them to draw or doodle on the paper for a few minutes.
- Have the participants erase part of the writing on the paper. Even though they try to erase their markings, it should still leave a trace of the original writing.

Comment: This exercise is a reminder that each action we take needs to be something we would like to be remembered for. No matter how insignificant actions seem at the time, they will leave an impression and cannot be taken back completely . . . even if we try.

Chapter 12

Who Do You Want on Your Bus?

Shortly after I joined Umpqua, I was in my office with my assistant talking about the next round of changes we needed to focus on, and an idea came up that I thought was intriguing. I asked my assistant to get the four top executives at the time to come in so we could brainstorm about it.

She went out to get them. After a couple of minutes, she poked her head in. "Can we delay that meeting for a while, Ray?"

"What for?"

"Well, they're having coffee."

"So? They can bring their coffee with them. Call down to the coffee room and tell them to come on up." I didn't see what the problem was.

She looked sheepish. I knew something was wrong. "What's the matter?" I asked.

Reluctantly, she told me what was up. "Ray, the routine here is that every morning at nine o'clock most of the management team go over to the coffee shop across the street and have coffee together for about forty-five minutes. And then at two o'clock they do the same thing."

I couldn't believe what she was telling me. "Let me make sure I understand this. They get to work at eight-thirty. Right?"

"Yes."

"Then at nine they go for coffee for forty-five minutes. And at twelve they go to lunch and probably get back at one-thirty?"

"That's right."

"At two they go out again for coffee for forty-five minutes, and then come back and work until about four-thirty or five?"

"That's about it."

Talk about the old stereotype of bankers' hours! Needless to say, those guys didn't last.

In *Good to Great,* Jim Collins says that if you want to take your company to the next level, you've got to get the right people *on* the bus and the wrong people *off* the bus. I think that is exactly right. People issues are absolutely critical when you are pursuing a strategy of relentless growth.

Sometimes it's easy to spot the wrong people, like the four coffee-klatchers. But who are the right people when you have a rapidly growing company? That's not always a straightforward question.

Some people think finding the right people means looking at résumés, job skills, college degrees, length of experience, and the like. At Umpqua, I took the view that getting the right people on our bus did not mean finding people with great job skills or long résumés. I knew we would be introducing many changes—a program of constant change, in fact, to build our business and make it grow. So I wasn't concerned with skills; I was looking for attitude—that sparkle in the eye that says, "I'm ready for anything." When people have that attitude, your company is ready to make the journey of continuous transformation. If your hiring decisions are based only on skills, looking for the best teller or fastest order processor in the world, you are making a big mistake. Hire based on attitude and spirit. You can teach people how to do their jobs.

When people have that attitude, your company is ready to make the journey of continuous transformation.

When we opened up that first concept store, I told Steve May that I wanted to personally select the people to run it. I talked to a lot of people in the company, not in formal interviews because I wasn't interested in their job skills, but informally, just to get to know them, to find out what made them tick. I was looking for that twinkle in the eye, the sense that they felt they could walk on water if they had to. And I ended up picking people who didn't really have much relevant experience. We were not trying to raise the level of customer service but to *change* it as part of our "what business are we really in" strategy, so it was not comparable, because it was so unique and different. So previous banking experience wasn't relevant: in fact, I saw it as a liability. I didn't want to have to make people unlearn things.

It wasn't very hard to teach these people how to greet customers, count money, make change, complete reports, and so on. But I don't know what we would have done if we had to teach them to genuinely like people and want to be helpful or to be enthusiastic about meeting challenges. Could we send them off to class and teach them integrity and caring about the community?

Remember Neal Brown and "The World's Greatest Bank" banner he put up without asking anyone? (I told that story in Chapter Three.) Neal was one of those people I hired for that first concept store. And it wasn't job skills or a long résumé that led Neal to put up that banner. It was his spirit, his attitude, his sense that he wanted the world to sit up and take notice. You can't give that to people through training. That's what *they give the company*. It doesn't work the other way around.

As Collins says, "In determining 'the right people,' the good-to-great companies placed greater weight on character attributes than on specific educational background, practical skills, specialized knowledge, or work experience. Not that specific knowledge or skills are unimportant, but they viewed these traits as more teachable (or at least learnable), whereas they believed dimensions like character, work ethic, basic intelligence, dedication to fulfilling commitments, and values are more ingrained." This is the philosophy we followed at Umpqua from the time I got here in 1994, long before *Good to Great* was published in 2001.

It's Not a One-Time Deal

Getting the right people on board your company is a constant, not a one-time deal. Think of a professional baseball team. Players have to make the team every year. Suppose I've been on the team ten years, making a big salary, but my productivity is starting to fade. And there is this young guy just out of the minor leagues, full of go, lots of talent, whose salary is a tenth of mine. You're the coach:

whom are you playing? I don't think people should think that just because I was on the team last year, I'll be on it this year.

Steve May, the first "right person" I got on the Umpqua bus after I came on board, recognized the importance of getting the right people in the right positions early on. As we were moving through the dramatic changes we were making in how the stores operated, Steve recognized that some of our existing store managers were not up to the challenge. Some didn't want to make the changes we were asking for and others lacked the ability to lead the charge in their stores. Steve announced that he was vacating all store manager positions—in effect saying they would have to make the team. Of course, the existing managers were candidates if they wanted to be. Steve met with each of them to discuss their interest in the store manager position and their future with Umpqua. The outcome was very positive for the immediate future of Umpqua and for each individual. Two of the six managers remained in their positions, three chose to leave the company, and one used her strengths in bank operations to establish the first centralized operations efforts at Umpqua—and proved very valuable in that position.

I am not saying that you should literally make people reapply for their positions every year. But I do think if someone isn't performing as well as we need in a current role, we have to think about a transition. I don't think it's good to toss people out who are really trying to sing your song. You should work with them to find another position where they can excel. Loyalty is a two-way street. But sometimes they may go sit on the bench for a while.

The other side of this is that you can't assume that people who were happy to be on the team last year still want to be on it this year. Once you've got the right people on your team, you've got to work to keep them there. You can't be complacent. When I hear about people who seem dissatisfied and might be thinking about leaving Umpqua, I want to talk to them right away—even if they don't report directly to me. I clear my schedule as soon as I can so we can sit down and talk. I hate it when we let good people slip away.

Sometimes it's just a bit of neglect—someone who has been doing a good job can get overlooked. After a while, they don't feel challenged, they feel like they're in a rut with no opportunity to grow. And that's not right. When someone has shown years of loyalty to the company—having Umpqua blood in them, I call it—I've got to reciprocate. If they're not happy in the current role, I work with them to find a better fit. When I succeed, I have someone who is more loyal than ever.

Sometimes an exec will come to me and say I've found someone great who I'd love to hire but I just don't have room on my team. A good exec is constantly recruiting, out looking for talent. You shouldn't stop just because you are fully staffed. You are always trying to build the team to win the World Series. Leaders have the responsibility to build the best team possible. It's a never-ending task.

I've talked at various times in the course of this book about my views on conventional wisdom. I think you need to strangle it in its crib, to be blunt about it. So I look for people who are willing to go against the grain, who are willing to challenge what passes for received wisdom.

Business needs more unconventional thinking if our companies are to survive into the future. Think about it: How fast is technology changing? How fast are consumer habits changing? How short are product life cycles in this era of high-tech? Business leaders will survive only if we are capable of thinking more differently than ever before—and if we are wise enough to attract talent that will challenge conventional wisdom all the time.

For many executives, people who challenge conventional wisdom—the type of people I call thoroughbreds—are very threatening. Thoroughbreds are great racehorses because of their high spirits. But their high spirits also make them hard to manage. The same is true for thoroughbreds in business—they will not settle for business as usual. Thoroughbreds aren't necessarily team builders. They don't get along with their peers. They don't go along to get along. Their approach says, "Get out of my way while I make it happen." If you can counsel them and channel their energy, you'll get outstanding performance. If you can't, they will leave on their own.

Give Yourself a Corporate Face-Lift

As Jim Collins notes, getting the right people on the bus is only half the formula—you've also got to get the *wrong* people *off* the bus. No matter how careful you are, you are going to let some people on the bus who don't work out. Sometimes it comes down to the fact that they just aren't up to the job, but more often it has nothing to do with their job skills—it's their people skills, their values, or their personality that presents a problem.

> ## When you fire someone like this, the freedom train passes through.

When you fire someone like this, you get a corporate face-lift. Things that had been stonewalled start moving ahead. A new day dawns. People start breathing easier. Morale goes up. It's a breath of fresh air. The freedom train passes through. People come up to thank you. And sometimes they ask, "What took you so long?"

Sometimes executives take so long because they're focused on their own convenience, as I explained in Chapter Nine. There is really no excuse for that. Yes, it's going to be a bother, but just bite the bullet and do it. Sometimes you're told that if you move so-and-so out, he's going to take three or four of his top people with him. My attitude is, fine, be my guest. So long. At the end of the day, the company is going to be stronger because of it.

I'm not suggesting being ruthless about it. It's important to help people succeed. You need to give people a chance to turn things around. You can offer them coaching and other programs. But at some point, the ball is in their court. You need to be able to say, "We've given you opportunities, we've provided tools, we've offered coaching—now, what are *you* going to do about it?"

Why Would Anybody Want to Work for You?

Of course it's one thing to say you are only going to hire people who will help your company to the next level. You want to hire the best, but what if the best people don't want to work for you? What if they say, "Thank you very much, but I don't feel that your company will be a good place for me." If you hear that often enough, it means you're reduced to taking pretty much whatever warm bodies you can round up.

In other words, if you're serious about getting the right people on the bus, you want to have a fine bus, a bus people will want to get on. That's one reason we work hard to make Umpqua a great place to work. For nine of the last ten years, Umpqua has been rated as one of the "100 best places to work" by *Oregon Business* magazine. This list is primarily based on employee surveys, so it's a compelling testament to how our associates feel about working here. In 2004, we placed as the number 1 best place to work in Oregon, an achievement that made me and all of us at Umpqua very proud.

Don't assume you can be picky about who you hire. If you want the best of the best, you've got to offer an exceptional workplace. You've got to value the people you choose and let them know it at every opportunity. You've got to empower them and provide opportunities for growth. You've got to be fair. You've got to build a culture that helps them thrive, that makes them eager to get to work every day.

A lot of companies say they hire only the best people—people with character, integrity, drive, and ambition. But in many cases it's not true. They're deluding themselves. They take what they can get. They're not willing to do the work needed to make the company a great place to work—a positive environment that helps people succeed. Sometimes, they end up paying top dollar for talent. They dangle money in front of people to get them on board, because that's all they've got. They don't get the best people that way, though. They get a bunch of mercenaries. And that spells trouble.

If pay is all you've got to motivate people, then you've got a whole bunch of mercenaries working for you. They'll leave in a heartbeat if they think they can get bigger bucks elsewhere. Every company has people who are there for the pay and benefits, the health coverage, sick leave, vacation pay, and retirement. They put in their forty hours a week and go home. And that's fine when the sailing is smooth. But when you run into a problem, those people are not going to be there for you. You can't count on them when you're looking around for help as a manager or leader. They will not be there.

The people who really help you grow are the people you can count on when you've fallen on your knees—who will bust their

> If pay is all you've got to motivate people, then you've got a whole bunch of mercenaries working for you.

britches to get things back on course when something blows up in your face. These are people who are not in it just for the money. These are people who get fulfillment from their jobs and from doing something right, who take pride in accomplishing something, who believe in what the company is trying to do.

To attract and retain these people, you need to keep them excited and inspired by their jobs—and that comes from a strong culture. I talk about building a strong culture in Part Five.

Being a great place to work isn't a matter of being nice to your employees. It is a matter of survival. If you want to get the right people, ask yourself, "Why would anybody want to work for us?" If you don't have a great answer, you've got work to do.

MOTIVATIONAL MOMENT
Do the Math

What makes 100 percent? What does it mean to give 100 percent? What makes up 100 percent in life?

Here's a mathematical formula that might answer these questions:

If you take

A B C D E F G H I J K L M N O P Q R S T U V W X Y Z

and represent it as

1 2 3 4 5 6 7 8 9 10 11 12 13 14 15 16 17 18 19 20 21 22 23 24 25 26

Then

H - A - R - D - W - O - R - K

8 + 1 +18+ 4 +23+15+18+11   = 98 percent

And

K - N - O - W - L - E - D - G - E

11+14+15+23+12+ 5 + 4 + 7 + 5   = 96 percent

But

A - T - T - I - T - U - D - E

1 +20+20+ 9 +20+21+ 4 + 5   = 100 percent

Chapter 13

Keep Your Board Strong— and Informed

If you want to grow your company, not only must you have a management team that can grow with you, you must also have a board that can grow as well. Change has to come from the top, and if your board doesn't have the vision to see the horizon, or isn't prepared to support you 100 percent, then you are wasting your time. Go find another company to run.

When I was interviewing to come to Umpqua as the new CEO, I wanted to make sure the board was going to support the changes that would be needed to grow the company. I told them frankly that I didn't know all the changes I wanted to make yet, but knew there would be a lot. And I told them there would be pain: "You will have an employee who's worked at Umpqua for twenty years, who is a friend and neighbor, walk into your office, tell you what a jerk I am, and threaten to quit." I wanted to know what they would do in that situation. "If you are going to call me up and tell me to go easy, people are getting upset, then I don't want this job. But if you can say, 'Sally, go back to work and talk to your supervisor,' then we're fine."

I didn't want to move my family from Atlanta to Oregon and find out six months into it that the directors didn't really want to endure all the pain and disruption it would take to put Umpqua on a path of sustained growth. I wanted to make sure they all knew change was going to be difficult and we'd all need some backbone to see it through.

Umpqua as a bank was just what I was looking for. It was solid, a well-run institution. I liked the size of it: big enough to have some resources and a reputation, not so big that it would take years of effort to make the sort of changes I was thinking about. It had a well-defined market, one we could make a splash in. But would the board really back me and the changes I wanted to make?

I had gotten to know the people on Umpqua's board over the course of several visits during the interview process. The directors were salt-of-the-earth people—self-made people, loggers, ranchers, farmers who had built everything they owned. When they said they were going to do something, it was done. When they shook your hand, you knew you were dealing with people of substance and principle. I was leaning toward taking the position and asked a real estate agent to show my wife and me around Roseburg. As we drove along, the agent spotted a farmer on a tractor plowing cantaloupe fields in the distance. The agent said, "You need to meet this guy," and took off across the field. The guy on the tractor was one of the directors of the bank, Don Kruse. After he got off his tractor and shook hands with me, we just sat there talking. I remember the moment felt like we were in an Old Milwaukee Beer commercial. The sun was going down, it was beautiful out in the fields, and I knew then that these people were genuine. I decided to accept the offer.

As it turned out, they always backed me 100 percent. I know there were occasions when they were breathing heavily behind the scenes, wondering what the hell they had set in motion. But they always backed me on every issue that came before them. Because of that, I had tremendous loyalty to them and I didn't want to let them down. I still don't.

As we started to grow and make some waves in the community, the board members were proud of our progress. If it hadn't been for that original board buying into the changes we wanted to make and backing them fully, we wouldn't be here today.

The point is that if you're going to grow your company, you need a board that understands what you are trying to do, supports it, and has confidence in your ability to deliver. You can't grow your company if the board is going to second-guess or debate every move you make. As I said before, we live in a real-time world. Things need to happen *now*.

Communicate!

The fact that the board promised to back me didn't mean they were handing me the keys to the car. They weren't giving me a blank check. I understood that they would back me only if they felt comfortable about where we were going and how we were going to get there. So when I came on board and started to make changes, I always kept the board up to date. I always tried to give them a heads-up about what was coming next. I communicated every chance I got.

We were in a small town, and news traveled fast. Board members had many sources of information about what was going on in the bank besides me. I knew they would hear about everything that was going on. So I had to be the first to tell them about changes, setbacks, and things like that. When the gossip or news did reach them, they could say, yes, we know about that. Or if it was inaccurate gossip, they could set the matter straight. I knew that if they were educated, everything would go easier for me.

I think that is a good strategy for any CEO to follow. Pretend your board is in a small town filled with gossip, that they're going to hear about everything, even if they're really spread all over the country. Go out of your way to keep them informed. Boards hate surprises.

When your company is growing rapidly, it's especially important to educate your board. Board members like growth, but it still makes them nervous. They wonder if you are getting the cart out before the horse, if you are growing too fast, spending more than anticipated, have the right controls in place, and so on. When a company is growing and changing on almost a daily basis, board members often feel they may be losing control. Some directors are prone to getting cold feet. They'll say, "Maybe we should slow this thing down." So I worked hard to educate them and point out what might go wrong, how we might stumble. And then if we did hit a glitch, they were forewarned. It wasn't out of the blue. They could say to themselves, "Oh yeah, we knew that might happen." The fear factor was ratcheted down.

We used to meet every single month, which was helpful as our game plan unfolded and we started to transform the company. A couple of years ago, the board felt that the game plan had become firmly established and we had developed a track record of success with it, so that monthly meetings were no longer needed. We now meet five times a year. We meet at the end of every quarter and again for a strategic planning retreat in October.

> When a company is growing and changing on almost a daily basis, board members often feel they may be losing control.

The strategy retreat is intense. It lasts for three days, and we bring in outside facilitators to run it. It's a big chunk of time out of everyone's schedule, especially when you factor in prep time. But it's worth it. We dig into everything, as deep as the board wants to go. In the end, everyone has a clear idea of our strategy and it allows us to go forward without second-guessing ourselves. If an opportunity comes up to move into a new market, I don't have to explain why I think we should do it—it fits right into the strategic plan. If I make a significant personnel change, I don't have to go into a song-and-dance routine to explain it, because it'll be clear where we're not performing on the strategic plan.

In between the scheduled board meetings, I keep communicating. I have what I call a board conversation, a conference call, where whoever wants to can call in for an update, and get questions answered. And of course, a director can call me any time.

I believe in getting our board together, face to face. We have dinner each evening before the board meetings. It's a great opportunity to socialize and get to know each other in an informal setting. It's another form of communicating.

I am very proud that we have so much trust and confidence in each other that we can talk about anything. We can talk about any tough topic that comes up and have rational conversations about it and move on. Once we were on the verge of a major acquisition and I opted not to do it at the last minute. The board complained loudly that I had not kept them as informed as I should have on the deal. It was a legitimate complaint. When the board says something like that to me, I'm guilty. I should have communicated with them better about what was going on. It always comes back to communication.

The Right People

It is just as important, or even more so, to make sure you have the right people on your board bus as on your organizational bus. Although Umpqua has changed dramatically—and *I mean dramatically*—since we started out in 1994, the board has evolved just as much. We've worked to build the board from one that had mostly a local focus to one where the focus is much broader and more strategic. And because of our growth, our success, and all the positive press we receive, we are able to attract extremely qualified people to the board—people who have great business acumen in specific areas, whether finance, data processing, education, or whatever. And that adds great value to us.

When it comes to boards, finding the right people means going after people who are going to be part of the team. You don't want to add someone to the board who doesn't get along, who is going to sidetrack things and create disruptions. You need to have a board that is caught up in the excitement of what you're trying to do. People who are going to stiff-arm your vision or the movie in your head do not belong on your board. We've had directors that have come in as a result of acquisitions and we could tell within the first two meetings that they weren't the right people for our board. And we were very quick to let these directors know that it wasn't going to work out, and they left the board. We don't want to get into a situation where we are debating among ourselves about things that are really management issues. Of course, governance sometimes means speaking up and challenging management—and that's okay as long as there is a fundamental agreement with the vision that has guided our growth for a decade or more. When a director does not agree with our vision, it is not productive to have that person on our board.

> When a director does not agree with our vision, it is not productive to have that person on our board.

Our board evolved naturally, bringing in new people regularly. We had a mandatory retirement age of sixty-five, so that moved about three people off the board early in my tenure. And as we completed acquisitions and mergers, that brought on new people.

Directors have to make the team every year. We have a board evaluation process—they don't evaluate each other, which gets too political. Instead, they evaluate themselves and then sit down with the chair, who interviews them and lets them know what their strengths and weaknesses look like and what they need to work on. All that information goes to the nominating committee, which decides who among the current directors will be renominated for another year. This is healthy. It makes it clear that the board is not a club, a collection of cronies, or a way to reward favors. Our board is first and foremost a professional organization.

We take board development seriously, as shown in the following excerpt from our Statement of Governance Principles, which is available under "Investor Relations" at our Web site, www.umpquabank.com.

> Directors should possess the highest personal and professional ethics, integrity and values and be committed to representing the long-term interests of the shareholders. On an overall basis, the Board should have policymaking experience in all of the major business activities of the Company and its subsidiaries. To the extent practical, the Board should be representative of the major markets in which the Company operates.
>
> Directors must be willing to devote sufficient time to effectively carry out their duties and responsibilities and should be committed to serve on the Board for at least the term to which they are elected. Each director should be prepared to offer his or her resignation in the event of any significant change in personal circumstances, including a material change in residence or employment that would adversely affect that director's ability to discharge his or her duties. Directors should not serve on more than three boards of public companies in addition to the Company's Board. A director's responsibility includes:
>
> - Learning the Company's business;
>
> - Reviewing reports and preparing for active participation in Board meetings; and
>
> - Attending, whenever possible, all meetings of the Board and the Board committees on which a director serves. Directors are

expected to attend at least 75% of the Board meetings and meetings of the committees on which they serve.

New directors will participate in an orientation program to acquaint them with the work and operation of the board and its committees. The Company encourages directors to participate in meaningful director education programs and the Company will pay the reasonable expenses of attending approved education programs.

Even as we bring in new people, we work hard to ensure continuity, both in the whole board and in the key committees. Some people just look at boards as policymaking bodies, which they are. But they can also be a tremendous tool and resource in helping you grow your company. We're not bashful about asking our board members to help in various ways, such as speaking at community events and helping with media relations.

Checks and Balances
Equal Accountability

In Part Two: Roles of a Leader, the first role I discussed was "Support Your People—and Hold 'Em Accountable." And that goes for the board's leadership role as well. The board's primary role is to support the CEO *and* to hold the CEO accountable.

Too many CEOs like to hold others accountable but try to squirm away from any accountability themselves. Often, they seek and obtain the title of chairman of the board in addition to their CEO title. This helps insulate them from serious board scrutiny. At Umpqua, our current chair is Allyn Ford, who has been on our board for over thirty years. I am not the chair. I don't believe in that. In fact, Umpqua's Statement of Governance Principles states, "The Board Chair shall not be a current employee of the Company or any of its subsidiaries." I think you need to have that separation from a governance point of view. When I'm talking in a board meeting and the chair thinks I'm going on too long, he'll cut me off in a second. I serve at the pleasure of the board, and if I'm chair, there is a built-in conflict. I am a member of the board, and as management's representative, I obviously have a great deal of influence. But when it comes to running the board and chairing meetings, I think the board's interest is best served by having that role in independent hands. It provides a good check and balance. In fact, we go further than just keeping the chair and CEO roles separate, as shown by this excerpt from our Principles of Governance:

> The Board will adopt appropriate structures and procedures to ensure that the Board functions independently of management. Those procedures may include executive sessions of the Board, the Board meeting on a regular basis without management present, and/or expressly assigning responsibility for administering the Board's relationship with management to a Board committee. The Board contemplates that it will meet in executive session with only the independent members of the Board at least twice per year.

When you decide to grow your company and are successful at it, you will be criticized. There will always be envious comments from people who are trying to tear you down. You get Doubting Thomases who wonder how you are really doing it, speculating that maybe something isn't quite kosher. So having checks and balances in place is important—and it starts with the board. When the board provides true independent oversight, it makes it much harder for wagging tongues to tarnish your reputation.

> When you decide to grow your company and are successful at it, you will be criticized.

Clear Boundaries

I work at the board's pleasure, and they can tell me to take a hike any time they want to. But they also need to know who the CEO is, and who sets the strategic direction of this company. I am not going to let them interfere in operational details. I just won't allow it. That's part of the process of turning the board into a professionally run group. I have people who have unintentionally done that. I've had to take them aside and say you can't do this, it has to stop, I won't allow it. If you have questions, you come to me.

We were in a board meeting and one of the directors, who was a good guy, didn't think our marketing team was doing a good job.

(Have you ever noticed how everyone feels like a marketing expert?) He had been complaining for a while. Finally, during one meeting, he brought it up again, about how he didn't like our branding. It wasn't on the agenda, but we stopped and asked him to explain his position. He explained what he thought was missing from our message, and at the end added this zinger: "So I found a marketing consultant and arranged a meeting and brought along one of our managers." He was going to explain how the meeting went and I stopped him.

"Are you telling me you had a meeting with an outside consultant and told them you had problems with our branding? And one of *my* execs was in that meeting?" I was very upset and made my feelings clear to the whole board. The chairman was sitting right next to me. He kept quiet and allowed me to vent for a while, and then lightly touched me on the shoulder. I was smart enough to realize that he wanted me to stop. So I stopped and the chairman said he wanted to say a few things and he told the board member that he had stepped way over the line into operational matters.

At the end of the meeting, that director came over to me and apologized, which I appreciated. It turned out to be a positive experience for all of us, because it drew a clear line between management issues and board issues.

MOTIVATIONAL MOMENT
The Vital Few Versus the Trivial Many

Everyone at every level at Umpqua participates in motivational moments—even our board of directors. Here's an exercise we did at one recent board meeting.
   —Ray

Our Vision
To become The World's Greatest Bank

Our Mission
The mission of Umpqua Bank is to create a unique and memorable banking environment in which our customers perceive the bank as an indispensable partner in achieving their financial goals; our people may achieve unparalleled personal and professional success; our shareholders achieve the exceptional rewards of ownership; and our communities benefit from our involvement and investment in their future.

Activity: Distribute one 3x5 card to each director.
   If the vision is our goal—our destination, what we want to be—then our mission is our road map to get there.
   Are you, as a director, contributing to the success of the bank *through the mission statement?*
   Write down two specific things that you did (since the last meeting) to move the bank closer to its vision. Many directors are very active in your responsibilities associated with the bank; however, have you ever carefully considered what has the most impact on our mission statement? When we review key performance indicators and relate them to the mission statement and vision, it's important that we are able to identify the *vital few* and separate them from the *trivial many* things that make up our days.
   Be as specific as possible. We will accumulate your responses into an informational list of ideas for the Board.

Chapter 14

Intangibles Matter Most

Every business naturally focuses on the tangible products and services it offers. How many units it ships, how many customers it serves, how much money comes in and goes out, how sales stack up against the same quarter last year, and so on. And make no mistake, countable details like these are important. They are the lifeblood of any business. But underneath them are things that are harder to count—nonmaterial items that you can't see, hear, or touch that nonetheless determine whether you succeed or fail, such as relationships, ethics, quality, and culture. The intangibles underlie and support the tangible products and services that businesses provide—yet many leaders give them insufficient attention.

In a competitive environment in which products and services are almost always interchangeable, you cannot grow your company without paying close attention to the intangibles.

Culture is such a huge intangible that I devote a whole section of the book to it later on. Here I want to talk about quality, values, and ethics—intangibles with a direct impact on how well you can grow your company.

Measuring Quality

I give several talks a year to industry groups and associations, and when I mention quality service, almost everyone grimaces. Why? Because—as the most overused phrase in business—it has lost its meaning.

If you ask CEOs how they rate the quality of service their companies provide, they'll all say it's great. But if you ask them to prove it, their eyes will glaze over in confusion. They don't know how to prove it. They'll say we haven't received any angry phone calls, or we got a nice letter yesterday, or we sometimes do surveys, but they don't have a *consistent* way to prove it. And if you don't have consistency, you don't have quality.

At Umpqua, we felt that if we were going to hang our hat on quality service, quality had to have meaning. It had to be measurable so we could hold people accountable for it. So we devised a PC-based system that actually measures the quality of service in our stores. And we have a crystal trophy that rotates around to the winning store each month. It is a big, big deal when a store wins this award.

Our performance was measured simply. I did not want this to appear difficult to do at first. I needed buy-in from the troops; they needed to see this as clearly different but fun. So we measured our cross-sales (sales of new products to existing customers) and started the Return on Quality (ROQ) program. See Exhibit 14.1.

The ROQ scores are all posted within the company so every store knows where it stands. Stores have to achieve a minimum score to qualify for incentive pay, which is team based, not individually based. Every store knows whether it's in the top third, middle third, or bottom third, and if you're in the bottom you know you'd better do something to get out of there.

The ROQ program is not designed to be punitive. The purpose of competition is not to create winners and losers, but to inspire everyone to higher and higher levels of performance. Our regional service managers use these results to work with the store managers in an effort to improve the team's performance. When a store ranks at or near the bottom for a period, the regional service managers ask a variety of questions. Does the store need additional training? Does the manager need more support and guidance? Are there personnel issues that should be addressed? Managers who are struggling with ROQ also reach out to other managers who are at the top of the list to get ideas on how they can improve their teams.

In addition to the store ROQ program, we have a similar ROQ program for the departments that handle backroom functions and other services that support the stores and other departments. The

EXHIBIT 14.1   STORE ROQ PROGRAM

ROQ was created to develop a ranking system to measure our progress in a variety of important service quality and sales measurements. The store achieving the highest ROQ for each month is presented with the prestigious ROQ Trophy in recognition of their outstanding performance. Each store's ROQ score is based on the following components:

Sales Effectiveness Ratio (SER)

The Sales Effectiveness Ratio (SER) is the average number of bank products and services sold at each sales session. For ROQ purposes, only the New Customer SER will be used to determine ROQ points.

Customer Retention (Deposit Accounts)

Measures the number of deposit accounts closed as a percentage of all accounts.

Customer Service Surveys

Customer Service Surveys are completed by customers and are scored monthly for each store.

New Account Surveys

New Account Surveys are sent to each new account customer. The average score for each store is then used to calculate ROQ points.

Telephone Shopping

An outside vendor telephones each store three times a month and rates the quality of service offered.

New Deposit & Loan Accounts/FTE

New Deposit & Loan Accounts/FTE is defined as the total number of deposit and loan accounts opened during the month. This number is divided by FTE usage for the month.

department ROQ results come from stores and departments throughout the bank ranking each department's performance on specific service commitments made by the department to its internal bank customers. Every associate who interacts with a specific department is encouraged to provide feedback—both positive and negative—to that department. See Exhibit 14.2.

Both department ROQ and store ROQ measurements elevate individual and team standards. The rating system encourages communication between teams and enhances their approach to resolving problems. Over the years, our ROQ program has heightened associates' awareness of the importance of internal customer services, built momentum for our unique culture, and motivated creative and unconventional thinking.

EXHIBIT 14.2   DEPARTMENT ROQ PURPOSE AND PROCESS

Every Associate Participates

This allows for the best overall feedback regarding the level of service being provided and gives everyone equal opportunity to provide that feedback. Associates only rate those departments that have provided them service within that month.

Electronic Surveys

The on-line survey program is easy and allows the user to complete it as they have time.

Allows for Open Communication Between Managers/Teams

Surveys provide you with the opportunity to have input that can help improve processes and services.

Positive Input = Positive Output

Managers want to hear about the good things their teams are doing, as well as the improvements that can be made, so that they know what works best and what isn't working.

Each month, the store and the department with the highest ROQ rating receive the ROQ Award, the traveling crystal trophy I mentioned earlier. It is a big deal to win the award. Kay Levis, one of our store managers, says, "People are just *waiting* for the ROQ numbers. 'Did someone get the e-mail?' they ask each other. We get so excited."

A major feature of our ROQ program is that it focuses on and rewards *team* performance, not individual accomplishment. This is extremely important, because it creates a system in which people hold their fellow team members accountable for results. Weak performers are identified and helped by their peers, not by management. Teams identify their own problems and come up with their own solutions. This is true empowerment. And it is what I mean when I say that you need to have systems in place to watch what's going on behind your back.

> If you experience bad service, it's probably not the clerk's fault, or the server's fault: it's usually management's fault.

Have you ever experienced poor service at a store or restaurant? Of course you have. And the first person to be blamed is usually the one serving you. But if you experience bad service, it's probably not the clerk's fault, or the server's fault: it's usually management's fault. Management has not communicated high quality standards, supported and trained people to achieve those standards, or held people accountable on a consistent basis. At Umpqua, we do. As a result, everybody at Umpqua is now a service critic. They live and breathe it, and they are very aware of bad service when they encounter it in their lives.

ROQ has turned into one of the most critical measurement factors in our company. Simply put, it's a way of monitoring the level of service we provide for our customers every day. Of all the measurements we take of our performance, this is the most important because that personal bonding is what defines the Umpqua experience. Our constant ROQ metrics ensure that we're providing the best local service everywhere our customers come in contact with our brand. Any company can have the same sort of program: you just have to make the commitment to do it consistently.

Values

As Peter Drucker wrote in *The Effective Executive*, "Any organization . . . needs a commitment to values, and their constant affirmation, as a human body needs vitamins and minerals." This is especially so when your business is growing rapidly. Growth produces all sorts of changes, in job descriptions, structures, personnel, policies, and so on. Communication becomes more difficult the larger you get. Values are essential to keep you on course even as everything changes around you. When you stay true to your values, everybody has something solid to hang onto as change swirls around them.

Many businesses have become fiercely competitive as they fight to stay alive in today's rapidly changing marketplace. Sometimes, in fighting so hard, they throw their values by the wayside. They forget who they are and become oblivious to what they may become—or have already become.

At Umpqua, we believe that staying true to our values has been one of the most important keys to our success. Years ago we adopted a vision based firmly on the core values of absolute integrity, extraordinary service, innovative delivery, and a strong sense of community. Since then our performance has proven the enduring power of those values. Over the past five years, the compounded annual growth rate on the market value of our stock has been 27.4 percent.

Of course, it's not enough to preach values. You have to act on them. If you don't act on your values, people inside and outside will quickly sense the hypocrisy. Values are only powerful if they mean something. Let me tell you how we act on our value of community. This value is not just about community relations or good PR: it defines us as a company and is integral to our brand and marketing strategy. It is *pervasive*. Umpqua began as a community bank in 1953 and remains a community bank today. Staying true to our roots, our strengths, and ourselves has meant upholding the value of community.

At its very core, Umpqua Bank remains a community bank, local to each community it serves, even as our network of stores expands. Three vital strategies ensure Umpqua's focus as a local community bank. First, as much as possible, we make decisions locally. Second, as I discussed in Chapter Seven, every associate is empowered to make decisions that benefit customers, creating strong personal ties that bind each store to its community. Third, our Connect Volunteer Network, a hands-on donation of time and resources, further cements those ties. Through our Connect program, Umpqua associates are encouraged to spend forty paid hours per year volunteering in their communities. We make it explicit: alongside FICA and 401(k) on each employee's pay stub, there is a line item for volunteer hours available and used. Umpqua associates spent nearly twelve thousand hours in 2005 volunteering at more than two hundred nonprofit organizations and public schools. These activities strengthen the fabric of the communities we serve—and show that we are committed to the value of community. The actions of our volunteers speak much louder than any words of mine.

> Values are like vitamins: they are required for the growth and development of any company.

As Peter Drucker observed, values are like vitamins: they are required for the growth and development of any company. But standing up for your values just makes good business sense as well. Your customers are more loyal when they know what you stand for. And the same goes for employees.

As we've grown across state boundaries, sometimes people find it hard to understand what we mean by our commitment to the local community. We try to explain it this way:

What Is Local?

You won't find it on a map. Local is not a place.

It's a decision we make every day.

It's treating everybody as if you've known them your whole life.

Local is not the opposite of *global.* It's the opposite of words like *careless, indifferent,* and *business as usual.*

Local is what we've always been.

Local is what we'll always be.

You cannot have a strong brand without a strong sense of your values. I'll get back to branding and values in Chapter Sixteen.

Ethics

Few things are more intangible than ethics, but they obviously produce real-world effects. When Johnson & Johnson stood up and dealt openly with the Tylenol tampering crisis, it earned enormous amounts of good will and sales of its top product soon rebounded. And when Ford and Firestone blamed each other for tire blowouts on the Ford Explorer and continued to pass the buck back and forth, both companies suffered damage to their reputations and the bottom line.

Doug Lennick and Fred Kiel, two researchers and business consultants, look at the connection between strong moral principles and business success in their book, *Moral Intelligence: Enhancing Business Performance and Leadership Success*. They write, "A funny thing happens when leaders consistently act in alignment with their principles and values: They typically produce consistently high performance almost any way you can measure it—gross sales, profits, talent retention, company reputation, and customer satisfaction. We think this is no accident."

Don't worry. I'm not going to preach to you about ethics. At this point in your life, you either have them or you don't. You know what feels right and what doesn't. Reading a book won't make you ethical. But I do want to say something about checks and balances and their role in keeping your company honest and ethical.

Just as checks and balances are important in our constitutional form of government, they are important in businesses, especially if you are growing fast. You've got to have the right controls in place so that you don't actually encourage unethical behavior. If you offer your sales team bonuses for booked sales, for example, you've got to have controls in place to ensure that bookings reflect real customer orders.

In our case, one of our largest areas for growth as we started out was our loan production team. Our loan officers were bringing in a lot of business. Now in our industry, when banks grow very fast, especially by making loans, someone will always accuse them of "buying the business"—making poor quality loans that no other bank will touch—and say that's why they are growing. I didn't want that.

I decided very early on that I needed to build a wall between the loan production team and the credit administrators, the department that approved the loans. The loan officers would be out there doing what they could to get the business, but they had to come back and convince the credit administrators—people who didn't work with them, whose compensation was completely independent of theirs—that the loans made sense and that the client was creditworthy.

The point is that you want to hire ethical, responsible people, but you don't want to leave critical ethical issues that can affect your business up to their subjective ethics. Even ethical people can feel pressured to cut corners. You need structures in place that provide checks and balances.

I'm a firm believer that if you don't do it right the first time and you stumble, you've got to go all the way back to the beginning and start over. And when you do, your credibility has already been damaged. It's much, much harder to get the ball rolling the second time around. If you don't manage the intangibles wisely, they'll come back to bite you.

MOTIVATIONAL MOMENT

Is 99.9 Percent Quality Service?

To help people think about the impact of mind-sets like "That's good enough," ask participants what quality level, expressed as a percentage of total items produced, they would accept if they were placed in charge of a product line or service—90 percent to 99 percent. Then indicate that some contemporary firms have sought to hold their reject rates down to just 1/10th of 1 percent (99.9 percent quality)! Ask them if they think 99.9 percent quality is adequate. Read the following statistics:

If 99.9 percent is good enough, then . . .

- 12 newborns will be given to the wrong parents daily.
- 114,500 mismatched pairs of shoes will be shipped each year.
- 18,322 pieces of mail will be mishandled every hour.
- 2,000,000 documents will be lost by the IRS this year.
- 2.5 million books will be shipped with the wrong covers.
- 315 entries in your dictionary will be misspelled.
- 20,000 incorrect drug prescriptions will be written this year.

Would you still be satisfied with 99.9 percent quality? Should our customers be satisfied with that level?

Part Four

Marketing, Marketing, Marketing

I've read any number of books on leadership, and I can't remember one that had much to say about marketing. Yet I don't think you can be very successful in leading your company on a path of growth if you don't pay a lot of attention to the market you serve and how your company markets itself. As I noted in the Introduction, HP cofounder Dave Packard used to say, "Marketing is far too important to be left to the Marketing Department." To my way of thinking, a leader's vision for the future of the company must be based on a clear understanding of what is happening in the marketplace.

In this section of the book, I talk about four critical tasks a leader has to undertake to stay on a path of sustained growth: understanding changes in the marketplace, which are often revolutionary, managing your brand, focusing on and serving the customer, and using design effectively in everything you do.

Chapter 15

Find the Revolution
Before It Finds You

I'm a believer in revolutions. They are out there in the market you serve. And you need to find them before they find you. If they find you, it's way too late. Think of Marie Antoinette in France or Nicholas II in Russia. Think of Kmart, the old AT&T, United Airlines, Kodak, and other companies now struggling to regain their footing after the competitive landscape shifted.

Big companies can invest billions and start revolutions, as Toyota did with the Prius model. Start-ups can get millions in venture financing and, if they're lucky, create something revolutionary, as the founders of Google did. Visionary founders can sometimes revolutionize an entire industry, as Phil Knight and Bill Bowerman did at Nike. But even if you are just a small company without huge budgets for R&D or angel investors with near-bottomless pockets, you can take advantage of revolutions. That's what we tried to do at Umpqua.

Revolutions Come in Many Guises

You don't need to create revolutions. Just go out and find those that are already happening. To me, a revolution is anything that is changing the industry you do business in, whether it's cosmetics or finance or pharmaceuticals. Advanced technology has obviously brought about many revolutions in recent decades. But many revolutions have nothing to do with technology. Design, for example,

> Revolutions don't have a big "R" on their sweaters. They often start small and become overwhelming over time.

is a revolution that is going on in my industry and a lot of others. Changes in customer behavior cause revolutions, as do new business models, government policies, social changes, and more. These changes can create opportunities for you if you pay attention to them—or threaten your existence if you don't.

Revolutions don't have a big "R" on their sweaters. They often start small and become overwhelming over time. If you see the revolution coming while it is still on the horizon, you can often take advantage of it. Our story at Umpqua is a case in point.

Before coming to Umpqua, as I mentioned, I ran a bank consulting firm and dealt with CEOs from all sizes of banks. I was struck by the lack of creativity in the industry. Banks were all the same—while other retail establishments were busy creating distinctive atmospheres for themselves. Many service companies were reinventing what quality service means—Ritz-Carlton, for example, the upscale hotel chain I raved about earlier. Retailers were creating a total customer experience in their stores, using music, lighting, and other design elements to project a particular image. You could walk into a Gap store and know that's where you were even if you didn't see the signs. Same with Banana Republic, Victoria's Secret, and so on. These were revolutions that were obvious in retail. But my industry slept on. Every bank you walked into was the same as every other. They all came in one flavor: plain vanilla.

But I knew that the revolution affecting retail clothing stores could and probably would spread to our industry. So we started revamping Umpqua by looking at other retailers, as I described in Chapter One. I think that it always pays to look at what is happening in other industries. Because revolutions can start anyplace, and it's often in an industry unconnected to yours.

After we implemented a lot of the retail and service concepts we learned from Nordstrom, Ritz-Carlton, and elsewhere, people started to call us revolutionary. *U.S. Banker, BusinessWeek, Fast Com-*

pany, and other publications took notice and started writing about us. We didn't have to invest big bucks in R&D or find angel investors. All we had to do was look around and see how companies in other industries were beating their competition. Then we had to get serious about breaking the rules in our industry, and then creating the discipline, sense of urgency, intensity, and focus to make the changes necessary. And in some quarters, sad to say, that's revolutionary.

How to Find Revolutions

It's hard to notice revolutions when you're in the heat of the battle because you're too busy fighting. And that's another reason why I say that a key role of a leader is to help people rise above the battlefield, as I described in Chapter Eight. When you have a wider perspective it helps you to see the revolutions gathering that can sweep you away—or, if you harness them, carry you ahead of the pack. But you can also use some specific strategies to sense changes in the marketplace that might turn into revolutions:

- Leave the building.
- Look outside your industry.
- Partner up.
- Ask "dumb" questions.
- Take your blinders off.

Leave the Building

In Search of Excellence popularized the phrase "management by walking around," and I'm a believer in that. But it's not enough—not by a long shot. If you are going to grow your company, you've got to do more than manage by walking around: you've got to get out of the building. Too many leaders are focused on internal operations and pay too little attention to the world outside and the revolutions going on out there.

The best leaders spend a lot of time out in the field talking to frontline workers and customers. Bill Marriott, the legendary former CEO of Marriott International, used to log 200,000 miles a year visiting Marriott operations and a competitor or two, according to

Fortune. "CEOs really don't listen enough," he told the magazine. "My ideas come from being exposed." One time, for example, he heard from hotel guests sitting around a hotel lobby that they would prefer to have tables, in addition to the usual easy chairs and couches, to make working and snacking easier—and soon Marriott lobbies sported tables for guests' comfort. Jack Welch of GE and Lou Gerstner of IBM used to make it a standard practice to spend more than a hundred days a year meeting customers to learn what was happening in the marketplace.

In setting the strategic direction of my company, I see it as a big part of my job to be constantly on the lookout for key trends that could change the way we do business. I make it a point to get out and about. Talking to frontline employees who deal with customers on a daily basis is critical. They can often sense changes in customer preferences quite quickly. If customers are asking for products or services you don't offer, bells and whistles you can't provide, or new ways to deliver products and services, your people on the front line will know it. All you need to do is ask them.

A lot of people would say that its marketing's job to spot trends. But in my company, that's everybody's job. I try to build watching for revolutions into every department's responsibilities. For example, our commercial bankers may come to us and talk about the needs businesses have and suggest how we can meet those needs with a new type of product. Everybody should be listening to the customer.

Look Outside Your Industry

We found many of our ideas for revamping Umpqua from great hotels and retailers. Most of the time, the revolution that will pay off for you is not in the industry you're in. You'll find it in another industry. You need to seek out other industries, see what their good ideas are, and then figure out how to apply those to your business. I guarantee you no one else in your industry is doing that as normal practice. You have a chance to do some really fresh thinking about your business, your strategy, and your market. Yes, you can look inside your own company or industry for new ideas, but most of the time, the truly revolutionary ones are from a different arena altogether.

Ask your marketing director, for example, to sit down with the marketing director of a successful company in another industry. If you're selling hardware, for instance, sit down with somebody who is in the transportation business. You may not get ideas about selling your product, but you could get ideas about branding, strategy, or PR opportunities. You will get ideas from somebody who sees the world in a fundamentally different way. And that is always eye-opening. For me, hiring bank consultants for advice is not exciting, because they're just going to tell me about trends in banking and what other banks are doing. That's okay, but it doesn't go very far. I would be much more inclined to hire a retail consultant or a hospital consultant to come in and say, "Here's how you can use our ideas in your industry." When you talk to someone who sees the world differently, you're probably going to discover brand-new ideas for your business.

Also consider reaching out to your own suppliers. Again, if you're selling hardware, reach out to the people who manufacture what you sell. How do they think about the market? What branding strategies do they use? Not only do you find ideas you might be able to use, you might also find ways to partner with them and generate additional revenue for you both.

Partner Up

Partnering with other companies also gives you a fresh perspective that can help you spot trends and revolutions. We are always willing to listen to people who want to collaborate or partner with us. Recently, Umpqua teamed with Rumblefish—a leading music-focused marketing agency—to develop the Discover Local Music project. Rumblefish reviewed the music of hundreds of independent artists from the communities we serve in northern California and the Pacific Northwest to compile a CD, *Discover Local Music: Vol. 1 Sacramento to Seattle,* that we feature in all our stores. Working with Rumblefish gave us a new take on the tastes of our customers. I can't say that it helped us spot a new revolution yet, but gaining a deeper understanding of the communities where we do business is all to the good.

Another partnering opportunity arose when Microsoft came to us, wanting to explore how their technology could help transform the banking experience of customers. Microsoft's vision included such concepts as enabling a customer's personal digital assistant (PDA) or cell phone to send an identifying signal to bank associates when the customer enters the store. In turn, an associate can immediately begin the process of accessing the customer's account to help reduce wait times. If using a bank kiosk, the customer could use the PDA to quickly transfer personal information to apply for a loan or other account services. Customers could also use the technology to transfer promotional information from instore digital marketing displays directly onto their PDAs. By partnering with Microsoft to test these concepts, we hope to ride the crest of the next technology revolution.

Procter & Gamble has an important program it calls "connect and develop" for finding revolutions based on working with partners. CEO A. G. Lafley says, "We want P&G to be known as the company that collaborates—inside and out—better than any other company in the world. I want us to be the absolute best at spotting, developing, and leveraging relationships with best-in-class partners in every part of our business." P&G isn't just looking for new products, but what Lafley calls "game-changing" ideas that go beyond product improvements to packaging, technologies, processes, and commercial connections that can change the playing field.

Ask "Dumb" Questions

Sometimes, when you've spent a while in an industry, you can grow a little jaded, thinking you've seen it all. It pays to get a naive perspective. People new to your company bring fresh eyes. They haven't absorbed the conventional wisdom that every company accumulates. They don't know what they can't do. They ask what might be called "dumb" questions. Next time you hear what sounds like a dumb question from a new employee, customer, or business partner, stop and think about it. It may only seem dumb because of a blind spot you have. After all, a dumb question is one that has an obvious answer, one that "everybody" knows the answer to. My feeling is that when something is obvious to everybody, watch out. There is probably a *better* answer out there that *isn't* obvious. And it could help you uncover a revolution.

And don't be afraid to ask dumb questions yourself—of your customers, your employees, people in companies you admire, anyone who might have something to teach you about your market and how it is changing. Even if you think you know the answer to a question, ask it anyway because you may not know the answer from the perspective of the person you are talking to—and that other perspective is often crucial to gaining new insight. Dumb questions are simple questions that probe the obvious and simultaneously challenge us to take our blinders off.

For Umpqua, "How can we encourage people to hang out at our bank?" was a dumb question because everybody knew that people rarely want to hang out at banks. The conventional wisdom was that people just wanted efficiency—to be able to get in and out of the bank quickly. Good service meant fast service, and that was it. But we asked that dumb question, and it helped us on our way.

> We asked that dumb question, and it helped us on our way.

People look at Umpqua and say a lot of the things we've done have been revolutionary for the banking industry. I take that as a compliment, but really, it's all a matter of differentiating ourselves. How do we stand out from the crowd? If what we do to stand out seems to others like it's revolutionary, that's a good deal. It'll get people charged up. But that's not what I mean when I talk about finding the revolution. Revolutions are going on out there that may have nothing to do with you, but it could be smart to tag along with them.

Take Your Blinders Off

Blinders are used on horses to cut off their peripheral vision so they can only see straight ahead and don't get distracted by things along the side of the road. It keeps their focus on the road ahead and their destination. A lot of people have their own blinders keeping their eyes pointed straight, focusing just on their goal, doing their job day in and out. They cut off their own peripheral vision, even though that can be vitally important in business. You want to take your blinders off so that you can get distracted. A lot of discoveries are made serendipitously, which means finding one thing while you are looking for something else. But you can't do that if you are so focused on doing one thing that you can't even see something else that is right in front of you. If you are intent on panning for gold, you may not see the diamond that lands in your pan.

My idea of peripheral vision is not just being able to see farther to the left or right, but being able to see things that might help me wherever I run across them, in a store, at the airport, in a magazine, wherever. Be open to distractions. If you run across a product or service that seems fresh and original or just incredibly good, ask yourself, How can I apply this to my company?

> Most of my competitors, bless 'em, don't try to learn from other industries.

I get most of my ideas from companies that have nothing to do with banking. But most of my competitors in the banking industry, bless 'em, don't try to learn from other industries. They don't seek out oddball ideas that they could turn to their advantage, and even when they run into one, they don't recognize it because they don't practice their peripheral vision.

It doesn't matter what type of business you are in. Revolutions are happening all around you. Make sure you find them before they find you.

MOTIVATIONAL MOMENT
Look Around

Materials Needed: Gather a random selection of items and place them on a tray (about twenty items is enough).

Exercise: Have someone carry the tray into the room, and allow participants a limited time to study it. After the person carrying the tray leaves the room, tell the participants you want them to list what they saw was wrong with the way the person carrying the tray was dressed. (*Example:* Two different types of shoes, name tag upside down, shirt buttoned wrong, things like that.)

Conclusion: It is easy to focus on the job at hand and lose sight of what is right in front of you. Be aware of everything that is going on around you.

Chapter 16

Your Brand Is You

Just as important as finding revolutions is maintaining your brand. If you've been in business for any length of time, you know that your brand is just about the most valuable marketing asset you've got. As *BusinessWeek* put it recently, "At a time when battered investors, customers, and employees are questioning whom they can trust, the ability of a familiar brand to deliver proven value flows straight to the bottom line."

In fact, the importance of your brand goes far beyond the bottom line. Your brand is about more than attracting customers. Talented people can choose where to work, investors can rate your prospects against others for better or worse, and communities can roll out the welcome mat when you come calling or slam the door in your face. Your brand affects every aspect of your business.

But what is your brand? When I talk to small groups, I like to ask people "How many people here know what your brand is?" And they'll say, "Well, it's a little tree," or "It's a moon with stars," or something like that. They talk about an icon or logo. But that's not your brand. Your brand is not a logo like the Nike Swoosh, an advertising slogan, a brand name, or any specific thing you can see and touch. Your brand is *everything* about your company that people inside and outside can see and touch. Your brand is you—your whole company.

Your brand is what your buildings look like, your Web site looks like, your products and services look like. I've told you earlier how distinctive our stores are. Customers can sit in plush chairs and get on the Internet and sip Umpqua brand coffee. They can browse our newspaper and magazine rack or watch the business and financial news. When they make a deposit or with-drawal, their cash or receipt will be delivered on a tray along with an Umpqua chocolate.

> Your brand is a living and breathing thing. And if you don't take care of it, feed it, and nurture it, it will die on you.

But our brand—any brand—is much more than that. Your brand is what you stand for, it's what inspires your people. It's how you treat your customers, your employees, and the community where you live and work. It's even what you do when you make a mistake. If you try to cover it up and pretend it never happened, that's part of your brand. If you admit responsibility, apologize, and go out of your way to fix things, that's part of your brand.

Does an associate say to a customer, "That's not my depart-ment," or is it, "I can help you with that"? Whichever it is, that's part of your brand too.

Your brand is a living and breathing thing. And if you don't take care of it, feed it, and nurture it, it will die on you. I pay a tremendous amount of attention to the Umpqua brand.

Be Yourself

Have you ever noticed that trying to join the in-crowd usually doesn't work? You might make it in, but you soon realize you aren't happy. You can't be who *they* are and still be you. You can't copy someone else and be true to yourself. It's the same with business. If you are trying to copy another company, no matter how suc-cessful it is, you are going to run into trouble. When you try to make your business something it is not, you've set yourself up for failure. You don't know it yet, but you're already dead. It all goes back to what I talked about in the earlier chapters of this book—your vision, your passion, the motion picture playing in your head.

If you stay true to those, you have a chance. But if you don't you will probably fail.

At Umpqua, we've always tried to be ourselves. We know who we are, make no bones about it, and stand tall. As a name, Umpqua sounds funny, but it's who we are and it's distinctive. What sort of name is Umpqua? It's a real name, for one thing, with a history and personality—it means *raging water* in the language of the Chinook Indian tribe.

We didn't try to become First National Bank of Oregon. We stayed Umpqua Bank, and it's the best decision we ever made. People don't like faceless bureaucracies. They like real people, real personalities. We started as a community bank and we're still a community bank. Over the past dozen years, we've grown from a small company with half a dozen locations to a sizable presence in three states with more than 125 locations. We've been rated the number 1 best place to work and the most admired finance company in Oregon in different surveys. We've been praised in the *Wall Street Journal, Fast Company,* and *BusinessWeek.* These are accolades that have strengthened our brand enormously. They never would have come to us if we had tried to be something we're not, or if we tried to run our bank like everybody else.

So if you want to build your brand and grow your company, you've got to ask some questions—of yourself as a leader and of your company.

- Who are you?
- What gets you up in the morning?
- What's your character?
- What do you stand for?
- What's the spirit of your company—fun, dull, strict, loose, what?
- What inspires your people?
- What makes them proud?

These are just a few of the questions that go to the core of who you are as a leader and as a company. How you answer these questions will determine what your brand is. If your answers go against the current, so what? Be who you are.

I know that some people will look at the questions above and wonder where I've left all the questions about customer preferences, market segmentation, and the like. But your brand isn't just a marketing tool, and your brand can't be the result of how you position yourself in the marketplace. Your brand has to go deeper than that. How you position yourself in the marketplace will change over time, but your brand has to be consistent and constant.

Be Different

Since you are your brand, you've got to be yourself. If you're not yourself, if you're just trying to fit into the crowd, you're not going to have a distinctive brand. Let me put it this way, if your company isn't unique in some way, your brand is bland.

To go back to our name for a moment, when you hear "Umpqua" you sort of think you can expect something different. It's easier to accept nontraditional behavior. When you see "First National Bank," you know what to expect. Everybody knows what that looks like. You've got the ropes to keep you in line. But with "Umpqua Bank" you expect something out of the ordinary. It differentiates us. People are drawn to it. A similar example is the First Union and Wachovia Bank merger. Two large banks came together; guess whose name is left? Not the acquiring company, but the acquired bank, Wachovia. Why is that? Because it's a hell of a good name.

Our name isn't the only thing about us that's different. Our whole retail store strategy sets us apart. We know that people are not going to change their bank accounts to do business with us because of an ad. We do advertising, of course, but we go beyond standard marketing—we call it "handshake marketing." We actually take that advertising and marketing down to the lowest level, inside the stores, inside the departments, and empower our people to do whatever it takes to blow the customer away, to make certain that the customer experience is incredible. The buzz and word of mouth this generates is tremendous and it brings us new business. You can't generate that word of mouth with advertising—it has to come from who you are and what you do.

We always have something going on that makes people talk about us. Our Pearl district store started a "Friday Nite Flicks" program awhile back. We show free movies on Friday nights and everyone is welcome to come. We want every store to be part of the community, so that people feel free to use their local store as a community center. Local stores have art shows, yoga classes, and book clubs, whatever people in the community ask for. Some stores even have weekly "stitch and bitch" sessions where knitters and needle-workers gather.

These sorts of things aren't marketing programs dreamed up by the head office and then rolled out as attention-getting gim-micks. They are a natural outgrowth of who we are and the values we stand for. We want our local associates, who know their com-munities, to take the initiative.

If you try to be like everyone else, if you are not yourself, you are not going to generate buzz. You can't stand out from the crowd if you try to be like everybody else in the crowd. You've got to be different to stand out, and the best way to be different is to be your-self. Some of our stores keep dog bowls full of water just outside the door for clients with pets. It's about having a good time and connecting with the community.

Some people say we're corny, but it's who we are—and peo-ple respond. When we moved into Northern California with the acquisition of Humboldt Bancorp, we wanted to introduce ourselves in a memorable way. We bought an ice cream truck and drove through residential neighborhoods and business dis-tricts and handed out free ice cream. It was so successful that now, at every new opening, we send the ice cream truck to the area for a few days or weeks (depending on the size of the town).

> We don't worry about being corny, quirky, and spontaneous.

At Umpqua, we don't worry about being corny, quirky, and spontaneous. In fact, I think all that helps build our brand, because everybody remembers it when you do something nice, even if it's corny. People don't remember the big things you do. They remember the little things. They expect the big things: products that work, on-time deliveries, and the like. They don't expect the flowers you send, the ice cream, or people bursting into song. It sounds corny, it sounds silly. But let me tell you: I love competing against people who won't buy into corny. I'm going to snatch their customers away. We're corny and people have fun with it. We get noticed and we get remembered.

Your People Hold Your Brand in Their Hands

Every time someone in your company comes into contact with a customer, that person holds your brand in his or her hands. If your representative ever says "That's not my department," keeps a customer waiting while chatting with a colleague, or just has a grumpy day, your brand loses some of its sparkle. Your brand is your company and it is also your people. That's why I spend so much time in this book talking about getting the right people on the bus, supporting them, empowering them, inspiring them, and holding them accountable. If you don't lay the groundwork with your people, you can try to fiddle with your brand all you want, but it won't get you far.

> If you don't lay the groundwork with your people, you can try to fiddle with your brand all you want, but it won't get you far.

We try to ensure that our brand is alive in every one of our associates. We have very specific standards that are spelled out clearly and we expect all our associates to live up to them. Here are some of the standards we consider nonnegotiable:

We will smile and acknowledge our customer immediately as he or she walks through our door.

We will stand to greet our customer.

We will consistently wear our name badges.

We will call our customer by name at least twice.

We will Deliver Plus One—always looking for opportunities to do a little extra.

We will hand out our business cards to offer additional help or to personalize our service.

We will thank our customer sincerely for doing business with us.

These are just a few of the standards we must live up to at Umpqua bank. Without them, the Umpqua brand wouldn't be what it is today.

It's one thing to set standards and hold people accountable for them. But we don't just want compliance, we want enthusiasm and commitment. That's why we work hard to both challenge and inspire Umpqua associates to take pride in themselves, their work, their colleagues, and the company. It's our people who make us extraordinary—and we let them know it every single day.

It's a two-way street. Our people make us unique, and that helps us win awards like Best Company to Work For or Most Admired Finance Company—and winning those awards really gets our people pumped up. People have so much pride in that! They are proud to work in our company, and they want to keep it shining. They do their best to keep it polished.

Your people make or break your brand. Make sure you support and empower them—and recognize and reward their efforts.

MOTIVATIONAL MOMENT
The Umpqua Tree

Try a variation of this with your logo or another symbol associated with your company.
—Ray

Exercise: Give participants a sheet of paper and ask them to draw a tree on it. Give them a short time frame—one to two minutes.

Conclusion: Compare how different the drawings are. Just like our customers—our fellow associates are unique and have individual qualities, skills, and knowledge that they bring to the team.

If you take a tree and trim and fertilize it, it becomes big and strong. That's just like our customers, who need to be treated as individuals with unique preferences and needs—making them loyal and happy customers.

Put all of the trees together, you have a strong and healthy forest. Put all of our dedicated associates together, you have The World's Greatest Bank.

Chapter 17

Serve the Customer

The goal in differentiating Umpqua from our competition has been to create an exceptional customer experience. So one of the first things we tried to do was to get our tellers to pay attention to customers. Seems like a small step, doesn't it? That's what I thought, but it actually took a series of changes to bring it about. I didn't realize it at the outset, but I would eventually have to change the culture of the whole bank to get people to focus on customer service.

When I first arrived at Umpqua, one of the first things we tried to teach people was to acknowledge customers when they entered a store. Think about it: if you're a customer standing in line and no one pays any attention to you, you get impatient and just want the line to move so you can get out of there. However, if someone looks up and says, "Hello," mentions your name, and adds, "We'll be with you in just a moment," it changes the experience. It seems like such a small thing, but it was hard to get our associates to do that. They were busy doing their administrative work—reconciling accounts, filling out reports, and so on—and since they didn't know the names of most of our customers, acknowledging them was out of their comfort zone. We tried pep talks and memos but didn't get anywhere.

So we decided to enact a formal program to help get people to stretch their rubber bands. What I was desperately trying to do was to give people the indication that real changes were happening. The program was simple enough: everyone in the store—tellers, new accounts reps, loan assistants—would have to take turns for a day standing by the front door and greeting customers as they walked in. Of course, many retailers do that, but in banking, it was unheard of. We had the designated greeter wear a flower corsage or boutonniere and welcome people to the store. When it was your day, that's what you did all day long. The program was little more than cosmetic, but it took people out of their comfort zones.

As with most kinds of change, of course, everybody hated the greeter program at first; they thought it was the stupidest thing to come down the pike in ages. But we persisted. We kept it up, giving everyone a lot of experience welcoming customers, making eye contact with them, and learning their names.

After a few months, as people became more comfortable interacting with customers, the greeter program was no longer necessary. We discontinued the program when it became clear to everyone that it was their responsibility to acknowledge our customers. It was a change in mind-set. Prior to the greeter program, associates kept their heads down working diligently on paperwork until a customer was practically leaning on the counter to get noticed. After the program, paying attention to and welcoming customers was a natural part of everyone's job.

But that wasn't enough.

Our associates were much better at giving our customers a friendly welcome and calling them by name. But they were still busy much of the time with paperwork or administrative work, which meant they were taking time away from serving the customer. Serving the customer was just one part of their job description. As long as serving the customer was a part-time job, we would never develop a great reputation for customer service. We had a situation where sometimes people would come in and get waited on right away yet other times associates would be busy doing something else and the customer would have to wait to get attention. And that meant we couldn't build the consistency we needed to build our brand on incredible service.

> Prior to the program, associates kept their heads down working diligently until a customer was practically leaning on the counter to get noticed.

You Need Consistency

No matter how big or small your business is, you have to develop consistency in the quality of your products and in how you deliver your products. If you are trying to create an image, buzz, or mystique within your company as well as externally, you have to be consistent. Without consistency, you are constantly going back and explaining to people, "Sorry, we'll do better next time." You are always making excuses. You can't say you are excellent at something and make excuses. This applies especially to customer service, when you are only as good as the last time I came in your store. I might have had a great experience a month ago, but now I'm back, and I'm getting the runaround, or the rep is being a jerk. The perception will be that you've gone downhill. It's the kiss of death. Don't ever put yourself in the position of asking or begging the customer for another chance.

I realized that if I wanted consistent, high-quality customer service, I had to make serving the customer a full-time job. If you want something done that's vital to the vision of your company, you can't make it a part-time job. If you make it a part-time job, you're going to get part-time results.

How many times have you walked into a bank where there's someone sitting behind a desk, busy—doing something—and you're waiting in line for several long minutes and they won't even look up to make eye contact? If you go to a typical bank, they'll have one or two teller windows open while other tellers will be looking down, doing paperwork. They are there, but they're not available to serve the customers waiting in line. A couple of employees will be sitting at desks, ignoring the customers as well.

There are two reasons customers are ignored in these banks. First, the employees are busy, filling out reports, because they have many things to do in addition to serving customers. That was part of our problem. Second, the ones sitting at the desk are likely supervisors or loan officers who are afraid to look up because the customer might ask them for help with a task that they are not trained to handle. And that was part of our problem too. In other words, at most banks, including us back then, serving the customer is only a part-time job, and the work has been specialized so that only certain employees deal with specific customer requests.

As I mentioned in Chapter One, when we determined that the business we were really in was the retail service business, I sent people on field trips to Nordstrom's and other places with reputations for superior service and asked them to report back. In addition to checking out how the stores looked, I asked them to look at how the employees behaved.

And they told me the clerks would greet customers as they came in, they would show them products and services, they would straighten the shelves after customers looked through things, when the customer wanted to buy something, they would take them to the cash register and cash them out, and at the end of the day they would balance out their cash register.

"That's it?" I asked.

"Yes, that's it. They basically spend almost all their time with customers. They aren't in the backroom doing chores. They're out on the floor."

So I said, "Okay, gang, that's what we're going to do. If we are really serious about customer service, we can't have people focus on it only part of the time and expect full-time results. We've got to take the paperwork and reports away from the tellers so they can focus on customers. And we've got to train everyone so they can help customers with *all* their usual banking needs."

That was the beginning of our Universal Associate concept. I felt that if we moved the traditional administrative work out of our stores and allowed our people to focus on serving customers, it would create a tremendous competitive advantage. It would be a major step toward creating a culture and environment that was centered around the customer experience.

So we set out to train everybody who comes into contact with customers to handle *all* the jobs a customer might want done, making deposits, opening an account, handling a loan application, accessing the safe-deposit box, and more. We took away the administrative tasks they had been doing and moved them to backrooms, out of sight of the customer—and eventually out of the stores completely, to a centralized operations center.

Some of our people thought that the Universal Associate concept would not be practical. If we took administrative tasks away from the frontline associates so they could focus full time on the customer, they said, we'd have to add staff to handle those administrative tasks. But that didn't happen. If you have ten people in a store only helping the customer half the time, you can actually get better results with five people who serve the customer all the time.

So we had fewer associates in the stores—and by centralizing the administrative duties in one place we were able to achieve greater efficiencies with the support staff.

In sum, what I thought at first would be a simple step of paying more attention to our customers required redesigning jobs, restructuring operations, and implementing a new culture where the focus was on customer service. At most banks and most companies, the culture focuses on efficiency, process, and controls, which almost makes customers an afterthought. Since we decided that while we were a bank, we were really in the retail service industry, I wanted the Umpqua culture to be focused first and foremost on serving customers, which was a significant change.

Serving Versus Selling

One advantage of the Universal Associate concept that I haven't mentioned is that it is an excellent way to improve sales. We created the Universal Associate position so that we could take customer service to a new level. Any associate a customer came into contact with could handle any normal banking transaction, from making a deposit to opening a CD or filling out a mortgage application. But once our associates became familiar with all those tasks and products, they were also in a much better position to *sell* them.

At most banks, if you go in to make a deposit to your checking account and ask the teller about opening a CD, the teller will then tell you to go sit at a desk and wait for someone to help you. At Umpqua, the associate can help you immediately. And when you've finished with your transaction, the associate can ask, "Is there anything else I can help you with?" and actually answer questions about home equity loans, deposit rates, and other products.

I am careful not to promote the sales aspect of our Universal Associates too heavily. I believe too many people in retail think only about the word *sales*. If you provide excellent service you will have the opportunity to sell. However, if all you ever talk about is sales, then you may not have many repeat customers because your commitment to service may be lacking.

I also felt that many people are threatened by the word *sell*. For example, if you hire bankers and ask them to help sell your products there is a high likelihood that they will say something like "Hold on,

I wasn't hired to sell, I was hired to be a banker." On the other hand, if you ask bankers to help provide an extraordinary level of service to their customers, they will almost always enthusiastically agree, because that's what professionals are supposed to do.

I never told our associates to be sales oriented. I asked them to provide an extraordinary level of knock-your-socks-off service, knowing that they would not be threatened by this, and also knowing that through great service our people would become comfortable with and good at selling. That is one reason why I never say that Umpqua has a sales culture, I always say we have a service culture, knowing that it leads to incredible sales.

> I never say that Umpqua has a sales culture, I always say we have a service culture, knowing that it leads to incredible sales.

Is your company set up to serve the customer? Is serving the customer a full-time job? Or is it something people do when they aren't filling out reports or sweeping the floors?

 MOTIVATIONAL MOMENT

Make a Face

Exercise: Using the Face Sheet (Figure 17.1), draw the emotions listed for each face using eyebrows and a mouth. After everyone is done, the team takes turns answering the phone with "Thank you for calling the World's Greatest Bank," using the emotions (sadness, fear, happiness, interest, and so on).

Comment: This activity is designed to launch a discussion about nonverbal messages and communication in a very funny, interactive way.

FIGURE 17.1   FACE SHEET

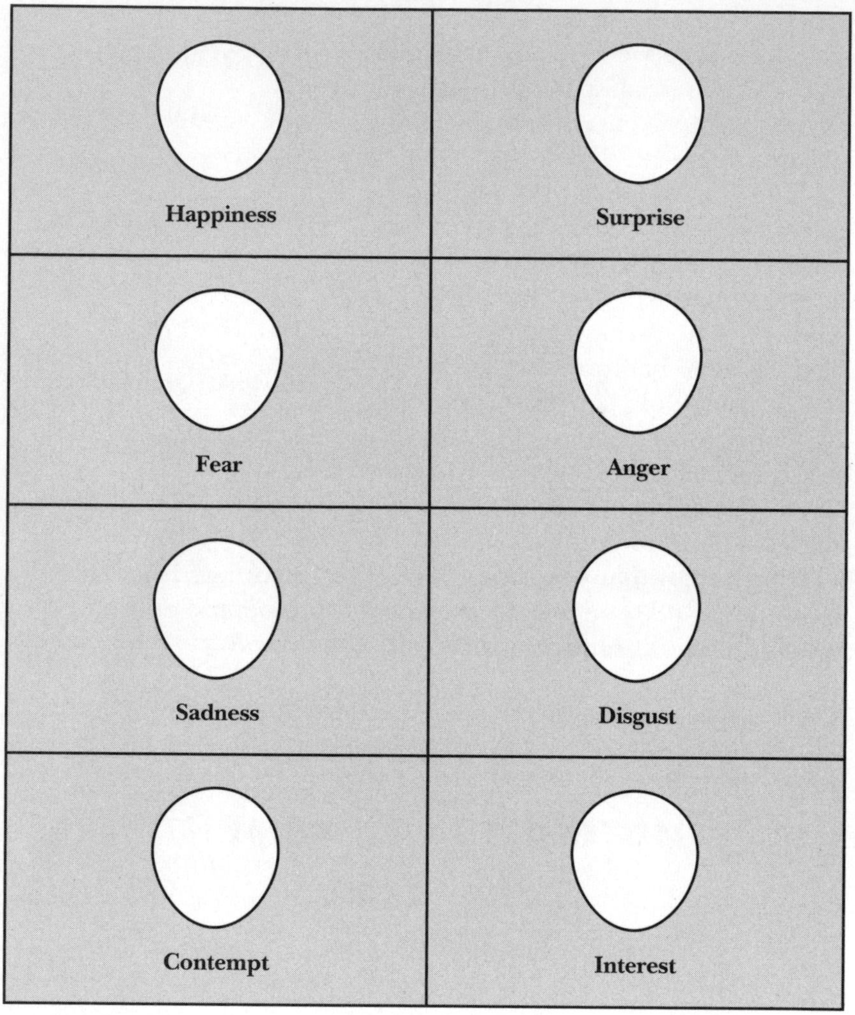

Chapter 18

Put Design into Everything You Do

"What is a chapter on design doing here?" I can hear you asking. "I thought this was a book about leadership. Why are you talking about design?" I'll put it bluntly: If you don't understand design and you compete against me, I am going to kick your butt. Let me repeat, I am going to kick your butt.

You can't have a strong brand without careful attention to design. As a leader, you cannot afford to put design in a box over in product development or marketing and hope it takes care of itself. As Tom Peters says (in *Re-imagine!*), "We think of designers, when we think of them at all, as odd ducks who should be confined to their cubes, far away from the strategy war room. Instead, we must invite designers to sit . . . on the CEO's immediate right at the boardroom table."

I think David Packard's line about marketing being far too important to leave to the Marketing Department applies to design as well. Steve Jobs, of Apple and Pixar fame, has said, "In most people's vocabularies, design means veneer. It's interior decorating. It's the fabric of the curtains of the sofa. But to me, nothing could be further from the meaning of design. Design is the fundamental soul of a human-made creation." Jobs clearly

> If you don't understand design and you compete against me, I am going to kick your butt.

thinks paying attention to design is a key part of the leader's job in order to create "insanely great" products. And he's not the only leader who feels that way. A. G. Lafley, Procter & Gamble's CEO, reportedly spends three full days a year with the company's Design Board reviewing the design of upcoming P&G products.

What Is Design?

Design isn't just about how things look, as Jobs said. It's not a veneer you lay on top of something—it includes everything your customers experience. At Umpqua, we pay attention to what our customers see, hear, smell, taste, and feel.

Of course, the physical aspects of our design are what show up most clearly in our stores. They're designed to be welcoming, a place where people feel comfortable hanging out, as I described in Chapter One. The comfortable chairs, the newspaper and magazine racks, the coffee, the local product displays, the computer café area, and the television all contribute to that. Each element has been carefully thought out to come together as a whole. We try to make each store feel like a community center. Even putting a doggie dish of fresh water by the front door is part of the design to make our stores feel comfortable and welcoming. Our design says that we are part of the local community, we're your friends and neighbors, we're professionals, and we deliver outstanding service.

But design goes way beyond physical appearance. Empowering our frontline associates is critical to our design. When people are empowered and take pride in their jobs, they can welcome customers with genuine warmth. The Universal Associate program I described in Chapter Seventeen is also an important design element in creating a memorable customer experience. Think of how different the experience is when you hear "I can help you with that!" instead of "Please wait over there and Frank will be with you shortly."

Design is being thoughtful, and shows up in many ways. The doggie dish I mentioned is one. Giving people their money or receipt on a tray with a chocolate is another. So is calling people by name.

When you talk about design, people sometimes think of designer clothes or sleek electronics like the iPod. They think it means cool and elegant. But it doesn't have to be. It can also be cozy and friendly.

People also think design is careful and calculated. But it can also be spontaneous. By design, every one of our stores has a special fund that any associate can tap into to send small gifts to customers to thank them or apologize for a problem. We surprise and delight our customers by sending them flowers or cookies or offering them a coupon for a free dinner at a local restaurant. Associates do not have to ask permission or fill out a form. All they have to do is write a check—by design.

Attention to Design Pays Off

At Umpqua, we are emphatic about the importance of design. And our attention to design has paid off. Microsoft recently chose an Umpqua store as the ideal setting for new video showcasing technology concepts with the potential to change the way people bank. Microsoft selected us because of our innovative approach to customer service and store design.

> You have customers, don't you? If you don't worry about how they experience your company, you won't have them very long.

Umpqua Bank's flagship store received a gold medal from *Business-Week* as one of "The Best Product Designs of the Year." The other winners were products like the iPod Mini, the Chevrolet Super Sport Roadster, and the Nokia 7600 cell phone. *BusinessWeek* said the Umpqua award highlighted "design's role in shaping consumer experiences."

You have customers, don't you? If you don't worry about how they experience your company, you won't have them very long.

As *BusinessWeek* put it:

As consumers grow increasingly accustomed to products that look good and work well, market-leading companies and their design teams must provide something more—well-designed customer experiences that evoke emotional attachment. . . .

Can such emotional connections be forged by design? Of course they can. Companies like Coca-Cola, Google, Apple, BMW, Ben &

Jerry's, eBay, Nike, and Harley-Davidson—as well as such lesser-known brands as Bose, Vespa, and Umpqua Bank—do it very well by designing great customer experiences. They have devoted fans who would protest if a product or service were changed or discontinued, or if a new product failed to live up to expectations.

It's nice to have devoted fans—and the reason we have them is that we pay attention to how we design the customer experience. Walk into a bank branch that was built in 1972 and then walk into an Umpqua store. Where are people going to take their business? Our numbers show that they want to do business with us.

Working with the design firm on our flagship Pearl District store in Portland helped me appreciate the value of design—and understand that it isn't just about surface appearances. Ziba Design spent a lot of time trying to figure us out. They wanted to know who we are and what we stand for. Steve McCallion, Ziba's creative director, told me, "We can't make this stuff up. We look for the essence, the values, and the personality that make up your DNA." They decided that we were all about "human centered banking," in their words. While other banks were focusing on efficiency and convenience, we were focused on delivering great service and helping our customers spend time with us. The design elements they came up with were not bells and whistles, not add-ons; instead, they grew out of understanding what we were really trying to do. And what we were all about (and still are) was surprising and delighting our customers.

The Customer Experience

Everything is about convenience today, almost to a fault. The convenience revolution has been going on for years and years. It's morphed from TV dinners in the 1950s to stores like Safeway and Whole Foods selling you precooked dinners. Everybody knows about that. What businesses haven't grasped as fully is that while people are into convenience, they are also into *nice,* into *quality,* into *cool,* into *fun.* That's sort of obvious when it comes to physical products like a sports car or the iPod. But it is just as important for intangible things like services. And for me, that translates into customer experience. Design plays a huge role in how your customers experience your company.

When you walk into a store, you have an experience. And when you talk to a customer service rep on the phone, you have an experience. Your experience can be bad, indifferent, good, or great. Of course, you want your customers to have great experiences when they deal with you. Customers remember great experiences and that builds loyalty.

Some companies, such as Disney and Ritz-Carlton, sell experiences directly. People go to Disneyland for family fun and to Ritz-Carlton for comfort and luxury. But every company creates experiences for its customers, whether it explicitly sells those experiences or not. Southwest Airlines sells affordable transportation, but Herb Kelleher didn't build Southwest on low fares alone. He focused on creating a special customer experience. Southwest has a good on-time record compared to other airlines, which helps, but it also makes flights fun, from the jokes that come from the cockpit to the attendants who burst into song. And all that frivolity doesn't happen by accident. It's part of the customer experience that Southwest has designed into its service. Yes, a lot of it is corny, but as I've said before, people appreciate corny.

Design for Competitive Advantage

Careful attention to design can give you competitive advantages that go beyond attractive products and services and great customer experiences. Design can also help your business become more adaptable and responsive.

We have recently developed a new store design that we believe will help us significantly with our expansion plans. The new store concept, called neighborhood stores, will integrate into established neighborhoods, providing residents and visitors with an engaging space to browse local merchandise, enjoy a cup of coffee, learn about community events and resources, and do their banking.

The new neighborhood stores are designed to be smaller, faster to build, and more flexible. The new design will reduce Umpqua's construction costs by approximately 50 percent and can be built in forty-five days. Typical bank branches take an average of four to six months to build. The new store design significantly improves speed to market and cost of construction, allowing us to build more locations quickly and provide increased convenience for customers. These stores will integrate into existing neighborhoods the way a coffee shop or café would, using smart design and technology to maximize space and reflect the character of each neighborhood.

The new neighborhood store concept can open within six weeks of securing a space. Key new features include in-depth neighborhood information and resources, a retail space featuring distinctive merchandise from local businesses, and comfortable booths equipped with computers and an electronic "daily specials" menu introducing users to neighborhood events and resources as well as bank products. The stores will also feature enhanced technologies like cash recyclers that not only maximize space but also enhance store associate efficiency.

> Today's consumer is looking for a customer experience that goes beyond needs.

In addition, Umpqua's neighborhood stores will feature a "Discover Wall." This one-of-a-kind interactive, multiscreen display covers an entire store wall and will deliver a choreographed video experience to customers. Using radio frequency identification (RFID) tags embedded in product information pieces, the Discover Wall will respond to areas of customer interest with personalized information and direct customers to more in-depth information and financial tools on nearby tablet PCs and displays. For example, if a customer is interested in buying a home, the Discover Wall will present information about area home prices—and Umpqua's available mortgage products.

It's a Revolution

Design is a revolution that is affecting everyone involved in consumer products and services. I think today's consumer is looking for a customer experience that goes beyond needs. If you don't think design is important, look at Target. A few years ago, Target was just like Kmart. And they've reinvented themselves. Their stores look fresh and attractive. Their merchandise displays and store layouts are pleasing and updated. Where do people want to go? Target. And Target stores are even holding their own against the cutthroat pricing of Wal-Mart.

If you and your company do not understand design, sooner or later somebody is going to kick your butt.

 MOTIVATIONAL MOMENT
Quality Check

Look at your work area. Does it reveal an organized, professional associate? View the store and department as a whole and discuss some simple things that can be done to improve the work area. Look at the area through the eyes of a customer. . . .

What do you see?

Part Five

Leading Your Culture

This section of the book focuses on building a strong culture for your company. By now, you certainly realize that every topic I have discussed in this book so far is a building block for creating a vibrant culture. You can't have culture without discipline, which I talked about in Chapter Two, for example. Discipline enables adherence to the values and behaviors that are part of your culture—and your culture should also reinforce discipline. If you don't have the discipline to live up to what you say you stand for, you will have a culture of mush.

If you've read this far in the book, you already know almost everything about Umpqua's culture. At Umpqua, our culture is made possible by our positive passion, by how we support people while holding them accountable, by making sure people have the power to take action at the local level, by the intangibles we measure, by our focus on great service and our aspiration to be the world's greatest bank, and all the other things I've discussed.

I think of our culture as our DNA: it is what makes us who we are. But unlike biological DNA, which each of us inherits and is unchangeable, organizational DNA is created, and it can change—and deteriorate.

I won't let that happen at Umpqua.

This section details some of the things we are doing to keep our culture intact, vital, and relevant. One of the keys to continuing to grow for the long term is maintaining the culture that made that growth possible in the first place. So the test is now that we've grown to more than $7 billion in assets and eighteen hundred employees, can we keep that culture as intense, as focused as it was in 1995, when we were just starting our revolution?

I'm certain we can if we put our minds to it. More than that, I know we've got to do it.

Chapter 19

Be There

Umpqua has more than $7 billion in assets, measured in financial terms. But really, I think our biggest asset is our culture, which can't be assigned a dollar value at all. Without our unique culture we could not have grown as relentlessly as we have. And our culture is what keeps us strong and growing. It's bigger than all of us. It makes us all proud to be a part of the bank and to share the Umpqua spirit.

From the look and feel of our stores, our Umpqua-brand coffee, and our line of Umpqua merchandise to our unwavering standards of excellence in serving customers and our commitment to community, we have established a culture that sets us apart and fuels our growth.

But we face a test every day.

Now that we've grown as big as we have, can we keep our culture as intense and as focused as it was in the mid-nineties when we had fewer than a dozen stores and were just starting our revolution? Can we keep growing and get to the next $7 billion and keep our culture intact and uninfected by bureaucratic inertia?

As we continue to grow, we will face enormous pressures to change—and we will *need* to change how we do some things, no doubt about it. But one thing I am determined not to change: our culture. Our culture is what differentiates us from the competition and our culture will continue to give us a strong competitive edge as long as we have the discipline to sustain it. (Does your culture give you a competitive advantage? It had better. If not, it's just a frill.)

We need to have the discipline, day in and day out, to do what is necessary to sustain our culture and make sure it doesn't get stretched out of shape by growth. At this point in our history, I'd say this is probably the toughest part of my job. But it's a challenge I welcome. It's not something I see as a sideline. I focus on it daily.

Where Culture Lives

If you want to maintain and enhance your culture, you've got to know where it lives. It's not in a plaque on a wall somewhere. It doesn't thrive in PowerPoint presentations or in company memos. And it certainly doesn't live in rules and regulations. Culture lives in the hearts and minds of your people. Once you understand that, it is easy to see that maintaining your culture is all about nurturing it in your people.

You've got to get out from behind your desk. You have things you need to do at your desk, of course, but you've got to be out and about so that people can see you. If your people don't believe in you, they are not going to follow you. And they won't believe in you if they never see you or hear from you.

Leaders build and shape their company's culture just as they build their company. Our people know the culture of this company comes from me, more than anything else. I'm the father of it. It's my responsibility. And people need to hear from me. If the leader isn't living and breathing the company's culture, no one else will. And if you're a leader, your people need to hear from you. If you aren't constantly demonstrating the values and behaviors that make up your culture, don't expect others to do so.

The heart and soul of any company is its culture. Your culture embodies what you stand for. It's the passion that gets you up every day. And that's what has to be communicated to your people. If you communicate that effectively, people will quickly understand what the corporate values are, what the heart and soul of the company is, and what the culture is ultimately going to become. You have to tell them what it is again and again and then set the example by demonstrating the values your culture embodies. Live up to what you say it is. If you set expectations, you have to live up to those expectations yourself.

We aspire to be the world's greatest bank, as I keep saying. It is a huge part of our culture: we aim to provide the highest level of service that our customers will ever experience. And that means that our frontline associates are critical to us. Their personal commitment to excellence in everything they do through creative problem solving, superior service, taking initiative, and sustaining our discipline is essential to our culture. So I am always out visiting them. I ask them how they're doing, what problems they're facing, how we can support them better, and I praise their hard work. Even as we've grown bigger, that job is still mine.

I was at a company rally a while ago in Portland for a promotion we were doing. I found a table where some frontline associates were gathered and asked if I could join them. We talked and after a while, one of them turned to me and asked, "Ray, when are you going to visit our store?"

"Well, I visited there not long ago," I replied.

"Not since I've been there, which is about a year and a half."

"You got me," I said. "I need to get out there, don't I? I'll come see you."

Constant Attention and a Sense of Urgency

I like to say that maintaining a culture is like raising a teenager. I don't mean that in a paternalistic way. I'm thinking in terms of the constant attention and sense of urgency raising teenagers requires. You're constantly checking in. "What are you doing? Where are you going? Who are you hanging out with?"

I've raised two children. Anybody who has knows how difficult the teenage years are—keeping the kids on course, out of trouble, away from danger. It's a constant worry and a constant challenge. The teenage years are when people are learning to spread their wings and are testing new freedoms. You want to support them and help them to use their new freedom responsibly. But you also want to set limits so that they don't get into trouble. You harp on values and setting standards.

And when you are trying to create a culture in a company, it has to be nurtured the same way you nurture a teenager. Of course, the most powerful effect you have on your teenagers, as a parent, is

> Maintaining a culture is like raising a teenager. You're constantly checking in. "What are you doing? Where are you going? Who are you hanging out with?"

the example you set for them. If you are not setting the right example, you can pontificate until you're blue in the face and it won't make a bit of difference. Same with leading your culture. If you are not setting the proper example, forget it. Just as you shape the character of your children, you shape the culture of your company.

When you are talking with your children about things that matter, about taking care of themselves, acting with character and honesty, naturally you bring a sense of urgency to it. If they are having a problem, you don't wait until some "annual performance review" to discuss it. You drop what you're doing and talk to them. You make time for them. And if you want to keep your culture strong, you've got to make time for it and for your people—and do it with a sense of urgency.

You have a sense of urgency with your children because you care—you love them and care tremendously about what happens to them. You don't want them to make the wrong decision. And you don't want them to make decisions that will limit their options in the future. You show you care by being there. By being accessible. My associates know I care because if they stick their head in my office, I'll stop what I'm doing and ask what's on their mind. If they send me e-mail, I'll usually respond the very same day. I do it because I care.

You've got to show them your passion! If it's a good thing I'm going after, I want to get on with it right away. If it's a bad thing that could hurt us, I want it shot down right away.

I'm constantly visiting our stores and other operations. I want to see for myself what is going on. I want to make myself available. But I am only one person and I can't be everywhere. That's why I've developed a number of tools to help me keep our culture alive and vibrant.

Create Cultural Ambassadors

If you are growing your company, there comes a point where you have to recruit ambassadors who can deliver your message for you. These have to be people you trust. They have to be people who really buy into the motion picture playing in your head—who get it, and who are eager to spread the word.

At Umpqua, we've created an ongoing program called the President's Club to recruit cultural ambassadors. President's Club members serve as a direct link between me and my senior management team and our associates. Most important, they also act as role models for the bank's culture. It is not easy to get into the club—usually only one or two new members are admitted each quarter. We have about eighty members now. The President's Club nominating committee asks for nominations from throughout the bank. After compiling a list of nominated associates, the committee contacts the supervisors of the nominees for more input. The committee then meets and creates a short list of the most qualified nominees, which is then voted on by the current members of the President's Club at their quarterly meeting. Winning nominees must receive at least 75 percent of the votes.

President's Club members have been incredibly helpful to me. We meet for an informal dinner every quarter. I tell them everything that I can legally disclose about what's going on—I can't ask them to be my ambassadors if I am not completely candid and open with them. At the same time, they are open with me about what is going on in the trenches, how new initiatives are being received, how morale is doing, and the like. I can keep my finger on the pulse of the organization pretty much in real time and get information delivered to me directly, unfiltered by layers of management.

Make Culture a Full-Time Job

As I said before, you can't expect full-time results by assigning a task to someone on a part-time basis. Our culture is critical to our company, and it is the full-time job of our executive vice president for cultural enhancement, who reports directly to me. The Cultural Enhancement Division is Umpqua's "keeper of the culture." Its mission:

- Recruit and attract talented associates who enhance our innovative customer service culture.
- Deliver culture-infused training programs to develop knowledge and skills in a way that supports job performance, professional development, and career advancement.
- Reward and recognize associates who perpetuate Umpqua culture through daily interactions, business results, and the ability to deliver memorable internal and external customer service.
- Offer rewarding benefits, both traditional and nontraditional, in appreciation of our associates' contributions to the bank's success.
- Be an exceptional resource and service provider for associates, so they, in turn, surprise and delight our customers.

As noted, the Cultural Enhancement Department oversees our training program, the World's Greatest Bank University. The WGBU goes far beyond offering associates the job skills they need; it provides them with an understanding and appreciation of our unique culture. Every new associate enrolls in several introductory courses that focus on job skills and product knowledge. But they must also take our Culture Orientation class, which covers the history of the bank, our Quality Service Program, general policies and procedures, benefits, and our unique retail culture. The goal of orientation is to help new associates feel the energy and spirit of Umpqua Bank and to learn how their individual contributions can enhance our unique culture. And since we realize that our culture is carried in the hearts and minds of our associates, we want them to thrive personally, and so we also offer classes on professional presentation, appearance, communication skills, time management, and other topics to help their personal growth and development.

Tools to Reinforce Culture

Culture also needs to be reinforced in many other ways. Internal communications should go beyond standard announcements and memos on practices and procedures and focus clearly on the values that drive your culture. Our "Culture" booklet goes to all Umpqua associates and details the six key descriptions of our culture (solid, genuine, exceptional, connected, resilient, and different) and explains how these key qualities work together with our vision, values, and mission to set us apart from other banks by offering a unique and creative environment in which our associates can thrive.

I recently began another communication program to reinforce our culture. "Viewpoint" is a message from me that goes out to all associates every quarter. It's another opportunity to let people hear directly from me. I focus on topics that are important to our culture, such as ethics, communication, and leadership, and our identity as a community bank.

Reward and recognition programs should also be tailored to reinforce the culture of your company. I'll talk more about Umpqua's reward and recognition programs in Chapter Twenty.

Take Culture Seriously

When facing competitive threats, leaders sometimes think the solution lies in creating a cultural transformation. They give speeches saying, "We need a culture of innovation," or "We need to develop an entrepreneurial culture." They think that changing the culture is like changing clothes. But your culture is not something you wear, any more than your skin is. It is part of you.

Building your culture happens naturally as you build your company. It's not something that happens separately. When we first started transforming Umpqua to focus on the business we were really in, offering exceptional customer service in a unique retail environment, we didn't know we were creating a culture. We just knew what we wanted to accomplish. We had all this change happening and we were focused on helping our associates provide an unheard-of level of service. It wasn't until we were three or four years into it that we finally started talking about culture. But of course, looking back at it now, we were creating the culture as we went along even back in the very beginning. We were training our people, setting high standards and holding people accountable to them, empowering people, and all the rest of it I have described. And it turned out we were creating a strong and vital culture.

When we realized what we had created, we decided we liked it. We liked

> **Your culture is not something you wear, any more than your skin is.**

> Every business has to create its own DNA. What is yours? What is your business all about? What do you stand for?

what was going on and so did the staff. So did the customers, and that's when we said let's put the pedal to the metal and take our culture to the next level.

I've talked about how we give tours to executives from other banks who want to see what we're up to. People sometimes ask me why I would do that. Don't I think they'll steal our ideas, our trade secrets? But anybody can walk in off the street into one of our stores and see the exceptional retail environment we've created and experience how well we treat our customers. Those aren't secrets! But that doesn't mean someone can steal them and get our culture.

As I've said, I think of our culture as our DNA: it is what makes us who we are. Just as no two individuals, except identical twins, have the same DNA, no two organizations will have the same DNA. It's true, bankers have come in here and taken pieces of what we do. But they can't copy our DNA. They've got to create their own. If you come in and take four or five ideas away and go back to your business and start to work on creating your own DNA, congratulations. We'll still have our DNA, our unique culture.

Every business has to create its own DNA. What is yours? What is your business all about? What do you stand for?

 MOTIVATIONAL MOMENT
Culture Word Search

Umpqua culture has many qualities. Some are listed at the bottom of Figure 19.1. Find as many qualities as you can in the jumble in the figure. Words may appear horizontally, vertically, diagonally, and backwards.

FIGURE 19.1   WORD BOX

```
L M Q R C T T E R R A M A T Y L E S M O P Z S D P
O O P G E N U I N E W G B C O M T E L P U N M F I
L E C O L A N L S W S G P E N O R I Q U A L I T Y
D E P G E R E H W A A O T A T C T E L E A M L E S
S A B A B E C G R E E C O G N I T I O N A N E O X
C H S I R N C B B D E G I T R H E R O Q I R C U X
S J U L A D E V U S S E R I E A S I M E F O A B C
C R I M T E R S T D E S P I N C T E R A B E A C A
L E A R I A L P I T D S O W B P A T O O L M F O R
R A N D O M D I T W E I V X E W T P N E C I B L O
P L A R N Z Y S O M I C F C I N H R A R A D C U L
A D C E E S S U R V K N X O W L E A Y S P R T I N
C L U M N S E R V I C E W D F S I N C E R E X Y Z
T E A V O L I U N O T E E R B R D I F R O E I E N
K K N P F G H L A T L E A I O U Y S M I F L E S P
T R P A B I C L I P E U N K N A B P E D E I G N K
P O T A G R E B R E O C N V A C C H M E S I C U R
A R T R A D I T I O N R O T W S S C T A S P E P T
S R T N E Y U O R L A T I D E R F O D A I W R F X
C R S A N H T N G U D Y A L E E J M E S O L I D A
D N W A R E T E R T U N T C H U R N U D N D N O S
J A Q U S B B C O M M U N I T Y C R L E A D R O W
S P U C V A T I W N T E H T A I H M L A L N A D T
B E B T A A C R T O S E D K T E O J H W E E L T T
B A N C H O L C H T T E C I H P S N B L R A S M S
O G D U M P Q U A N O D W I F S I H P M R E O D O
N T Y U O M E A E T T L E L C F S O E R B A E I O
U W Y S X Q U M R S O M C U L T E W V A E I W I H
S M A P W J T L U D I J E Q U P T R D N T K L M N
I W T E R I O R D I N A X I D A D Y E U L O O F T
I P Q X M E I C N T D J T M I S S I O N I S M A H
B L E M V G H T I T E P R A D A N S U I T H T A T
T H O M N R E Y T M K E A P U C O S R O E Z L E C
U C O N N E C T E D U Y O B L E W V I T A C R T N
L U I S F A C Y R R M W R T H I I D E S M U I T S
P L R Y D T A I D F N E D Y L T N U P B L S E W A
A I N D R F F A R T D V I S I Q N U M P Q V L L C
E U X D E S D I N B R A N V I C E S I N U U A L I
B R A P D T F F I T Y I A O N A R Y R E W A S S I
W E L C O M E B C K C T R R S O S G N E U I N E D
M I W G B V O L U C U L Y T C O M M G R E A D O N
```

action	different	people	ROQ	tradition
brag	exceptional	professional	service	umpqua bank
celebration	extraordinary	quality	sincere	values
commitment	genuine	random	smile	volunteer
community	greatest	recognition	solid	welcome
connected	growth	resilient	spirit	winners
culture	mission	rewards	team	WGBU

Chapter 20

Keep Your Balance

Staying on a path of sustained growth is like walking on a tightrope. You always have to keep your balance. We've recently seen a number of companies that seemed to be experiencing solid growth run into real trouble. A lot of the time their cultures were seriously out of balance and off-kilter. Think Enron—but there are many others, a lot of which don't make the news.

I believe balance is important. And keeping your balance involves many dimensions. You have to balance work with play. You have to balance communication, keeping it two-way. You have to balance the interests of all the stakeholders in your company. (One of those stakeholders is the community where you do business; staying connected with the community is an important anchor for balance that I always emphasize.) And you have to balance your needs today with your needs tomorrow. A balanced culture helps you keep your company on course.

Have Fun

Too many people believe if you're serious about business you can't have fun. They think business and fun go in two different directions. "I mean business" tells people to take things seriously. But why shouldn't business be fun? At Umpqua, we mean business and we aim to have fun with it too. If you can't have fun at work, things are going to get out of balance pretty quickly.

Even in our industry, which is known for being stuffy, you should be able to have fun. I tell people you should be able to have a good time at work. That's one of the reasons we do our motivational moments, so people have a good time, laugh a little, and start the day with their batteries fully charged.

As I've said, we have motivational moments every morning throughout the company. Every day, every single team in every department or store in this company has a five-minute motivational moment. When we started doing this in 1995, I said I wanted everybody to get together for a few minutes at the start of the day to do something fun and interesting. I told them, "I don't care what you talk about, but it can't be operational. It needs to get people fired up for the day. Let's have a little bit of fun before the day starts."

Motivational moments are a big part of our culture, our DNA. (You've seen examples of what we do throughout this book.) I've told people, failure to do your motivational moments is grounds for immediate dismissal. I don't care how good you are at producing numbers, I will dismiss you if you don't live up to our standards. Even in my office, we have motivational moments every single morning. Some managers in the past have said that their units are just too busy to take the time to do their motivational moments. But I tell them, you are not allowed to use work as an excuse to avoid having fun. Bring your people together, do something different, get jazzed up, and have fun! It only takes five minutes!

Empower your people so they can have fun—and have fun with them. I'm not the best example of this, but leaders should let their hair down once in a while. I'm seen as a kind of intense, stone-faced guy, but I do my best to get out there and let loose with the troops. They just love it when you do.

> Having fun loosens people up, gets the creative juices flowing, and makes the job ahead seem less daunting.

Having fun is *good* for business! Having fun loosens people up, gets the creative juices flowing, and makes the job ahead seem less daunting. And *your customers* like it when you are having fun.

When I was in Roseburg early on, we were remodeling the office I used, so I sat out in the lobby of the Roseburg

> Where would you like to take your business? To someplace that makes you smile, or to someplace where people are bored or stressed out?

store for a couple of months—what an eye-opener! I observed the associates have their motivational moments every morning and they were less than inspiring. After watching this for a while, I took the store manager aside and asked her, "Can I give you an idea for a motivational moment?" She said sure. "You know the Rolling Stones song, *Start Me Up?*" She did. "Well, get a CD with that on it, and bring it in tomorrow, but don't tell anybody about it." So the next day she brought it in, and I told her to put it on the audio system, and crank the volume all the way up, almost as high as it would go. That whole building shook! And of course everybody started dancing and having fun. And when I looked out the door, out on the sidewalk were three or four customers who'd been waiting for the doors to open, also dancing along.

Ever since then, after letting people know it's okay to get a little rowdy and have fun, that store has had great motivational moments.

Think about it: Where would you like to take your business? To someplace that makes you smile, or to someplace where people are bored or stressed out? When people are allowed to have fun at work, they won't be bored and their stress levels are reduced. Southwest Airlines is famous for this. Their employees make jokes, play tricks like hiding in the overhead luggage compartments, and the passengers get a big laugh out of it.

Celebrate!

I think that it's important to celebrate—it's another way to stay balanced. Our associates work hard and it's important to recognize and celebrate their accomplishments. Every year we conduct what we call our Celebration of Excellence. This is our award ceremony to recognize our associates for their great work and commitment to our culture. It's a big deal for us—our version of the Academy Awards. We start out with a catered reception, do the award show, and conclude with dinner and dancing. For the award show, we hire a professional master of ceremonies, normally a comedian who gets the crowd charged up and laughing. A live band provides the music. Our people wear black tie and evening gowns. The awards we present are gold statues that resemble Oscars. We really pull out all the stops for this event because that's what our associates deserve—we celebrate them.

Our Celebration of Excellence focuses on our associates who work on the front lines. We don't give awards to executive management. We keep the spotlight on our associates and the hard work they've done, with awards like Rookie of the Year, Store Associate of the Year, Department Associate of the Year, Team of the Year, the Culture Award, Random Acts of Extraordinary Service, and the like. I like to see a lot of people up on that stage, in the spotlight, winning Umpqua's version of the Academy Award. It's all about giving them that recognition. We tell them they are the ones who make Umpqua the world's greatest bank. And people are really proud when they win or when they see their coworkers win.

We keep the Celebration of Excellence focused on our associates, as I said, but we also keep it focused on our values, our culture. A lot of companies focus too much on money and give out awards like Top Salesman of the Year, or Top Producer. We don't. Profits are important, of course, but it's our culture that produces the profits, so that is what we celebrate. It's another way of staying balanced.

When you do it right and keep the focus on your culture, a celebration is a way to rejuvenate everything you stand for. After a year of hard work, it's like a cool shower that wakes people up and refreshes them. If you plan the celebration well, hit the right notes, the people who attend will say: *Now I understand what we are all about, what we're doing here. This is cool.* When a new employee attends our Celebration of Excellence for the first time, all the talk they've heard about our culture comes to life—they can see it and feel it. It gives people who may be a bit weary a shot in the arm. It lets the people who put their heart and soul into their job and always go the extra mile say to themselves, now I know why I did it *and* it was worth it. And for people who may be sitting on the fence, wondering whether they want a career with us, it makes it easier for them to make that decision. In just a few hours once a year through our Celebration of Excellence, we create a renewing process that reinforces what we stand for.

Balance the Interests of Your Stakeholders

To stay balanced, every company has to consider four groups of stakeholders: customers, employees, shareholders, and the wider community. All four need proper attention. Yet some companies shortchange employees to benefit shareholders. Others do the exact opposite—pampering top executives with bonuses while stock prices stagnate. All too many companies, unfortunately, shortchange the communities where they do business with scarcely a second thought. And of course, some companies bilk their customers with shoddy products or poor service.

Such unbalanced companies might do well for a while, but I firmly believe that whatever success they might achieve is transitory, because it's not built on a solid foundation. Solid companies, with solid long-term growth, have cultures that emphasize treating all four stakeholder groups fairly. They keep themselves balanced.

At Umpqua, we have built all four groups into our mission statement, to keep them front and center at all times. Our mission is straightforward:

> The mission of Umpqua Bank is to create a unique and memorable banking environment in which OUR CUSTOMERS perceive the bank as an indispensable partner in achieving their financial goals; OUR PEOPLE may achieve unparalleled personal and professional success; OUR SHAREHOLDERS achieve the exceptional rewards of ownership; and OUR COMMUNITIES benefit from our involvement and investment in the future.

I have already discussed at length how we focus on our customers, and how we empower our associates. You can find out how our shareholders have fared by looking up our stock symbol (UMPQ) on the Internet. In this chapter, I want to talk about how we connect with the communities we serve. It's an important part of our story.

Connection

We work hard to make sure we stay connected to the communities where we do business. When you are connected to the larger community, it anchors you in solid ground and that helps keep you balanced. Like many companies, we support the communities we serve through charitable donations—but writing a check doesn't do much to connect you to the community all by itself. We do more.

We have always encouraged associates to volunteer in local programs. In 2004, however, we decided to go beyond encouragement and put resources in place to provide paid time off that associates can use to volunteer. We launched the Umpqua Bank Connect Volunteer Network, as I described in Chapter Fourteen. By encouraging our people to volunteer during work hours, we are making a concrete commitment to staying connected to our communities. Whether it's time assisting a kindergarten class, mentoring a troubled teen, or helping build a new home for a family, we share in the work of strengthening communities.

Another way we stay connected to our communities is with local advisory boards. We are involved in many local communities in regions up and down the West Coast. So we have created advisory boards made up of business and community leaders in the communities we serve. We meet with them three or four times a year. Their job is to help us understand what is going on in the community, what we should be paying attention to—and to constantly give us feedback on how we are doing in their community and what we are not doing that we should be doing. That's invaluable for a company that wants to grow. When you're spread out over a lot of different areas, you can lose touch. Having these community boards helps you stay in touch and provides an early warning system for developments that may threaten you. The boards also help us maintain our commitment to remain a community bank even as we grow.

Community involvement is not just good public relations. It gets people to look outside the walls of our company to the larger world. It helps us keep things in perspective. We avoid a myopic focus on ourselves. As I've noted, we do a lot to celebrate ourselves and our culture. If that is all we did, we could become too inwardly focused.

Balanced Communication

Too often in companies, communication goes only one way, and you know what direction that is: top down. Balanced communication goes both ways.

Communication is a tricky thing—not because it's tough to express everything you want to say clearly and concisely, but because someone on the other end is always interpreting everything you're saying. To communicate effectively, you've got to make sure you've been understood, and that means listening. Good managers listen at least as much as they talk. They ask questions and listen intently to the answers.

Managers and subordinates often have trouble communicating because of a perceived power differential between them. How often have you seen this situation? A manager calls someone into the office to discuss an issue. At the end of the meeting, the subordinate walks out of the office and the boss thinks, "Well I certainly cleared that up." Back at his or her desk, the subordinate thinks, "I still don't know what my boss expects me to do." That happens all the time. Often the biggest problem with communication comes from managers or leaders who think the person on the other side of the table understood what was said. Meanwhile, the other person walks out of the meeting wondering what it was all about.

Recently, I asked one of my execs to make sure the people in a division of a recently acquired company were engaged. It was an important part of our reason for the acquisition so I asked him to make sure they were well taken care of, knew that we valued them, and that they understood that. He said he'd take care of it. I got a couple of e-mails later on explaining how well things were going. And then things fell apart, some key people started making noises about moving on. I called him in and asked what was going on. He said he couldn't figure it out. "We had a great meeting," he told me.

"No," I said. "*You* had a great meeting. To *them* it was a lousy meeting."

You've got to open your ears to what people are really trying to tell you. More than that, you've got to dig for it. If I walk into someone's office and ask, "How are you doing?" and they say unenthusiastically, "Oh, things are okay," I'm going to close the door and ask, "What's going on? What's bothering you?" You've got to dig. Too many leaders have so much on their plates, they don't want to hear the problems. A lackluster statement that things are okay is good enough for them. They don't want another issue to deal with. And the other person thinks, *My boss doesn't care how I feel.*

Dig deeper. Peel back the layers. I get impatient with managers who don't want to spend the time to peel back the layers and find out what is really going on. And then they're surprised when they get hit with something they didn't expect.

Here's a tip to ensure clear two-way communication with the people who report to you: After discussing an issue and thinking you've reached closure, circle back four hours later. Ask, "Are you okay with our discussion? Is everything cleared up? Is anything bothering you?" Give people a chance to come back to you and tell you if they still have questions or concerns. Often as not, you'll find they've told you they understood and everything was cleared up because that's what they thought you wanted to hear.

> Often as not, you'll find they've told you they understood and everything was cleared up because that's what they thought you wanted to hear.

Short Term Versus Long Term

Balancing the need for short-term results with the goals of long-term growth is a problem with many companies. If you are leading your company for growth, you've always got to keep your eyes on the long term even as you manage day-to-day operations. Keep your eyes on the horizon. You want to make sure that every decision you make is getting you closer to where you want to go.

Every public company faces pressure to produce short-term results—and too many leaders give in to that pressure. I resist that pressure. For example, to keep stock analysts happy, a lot of companies choose to give quarterly guidance about earnings expectations. We don't. We do have conference calls with analysts every quarter, but we tell them what we *did*. We want to keep them informed, but we don't tell them what we expect to do. We don't want to lock ourselves into running the company on a quarterly basis. We try to keep our eyes focused on where we want to go, on the horizon, on our never-ending journey.

We may even make decisions that hurt earnings for the next quarter or two, if the long-term impact of the decision is in the best interests of our shareholders. The analysts always seem to focus on "What are you going to do for me right now?" I can't afford to think like that and I don't want to put myself in the position where I feel pressured to cut the marketing budget, for example, so I can add a penny per share to earnings next quarter. Why would I put myself in that position? It's stupid. You are better off explaining why you are a penny short.

A Never-Ending Journey

I said early on in this book that leading your company for growth is a never-ending journey. To keep yourself on that path, do what the tightrope walker does. Stay balanced by keeping your eyes on the horizon.

 MOTIVATIONAL MOMENT
Play It Loud!

Play a favorite rock and roll song and have everyone stand up and do a few aerobic exercises. It gets the group up and moving together and there's generally laughter involved. It also helps rejuvenate everyone and gives you a jump on the rest of the day.

Chapter 21

Remember
Who You Are

You'll see a lot of books about leading and managing change. You'll also see books like *Who Moved My Cheese,* designed to help employees deal positively with change. What gets short shrift, in my opinion, is staying on track. We've gone through a lot of changes at Umpqua, and as I have said before, growing your company is a never-ending process of change. As you know by now, I think change can be incredibly positive. But you've also got to know what *not* to change—what to maintain if you want to stay on track. And you've got to pay attention to those things to make sure they don't get stretched out of shape by growth.

The biggest danger of relentless growth is that your very growth will undermine the qualities that produced that success in the first place. We started out as sort of an underdog—a small company in an industry dominated by companies a hundred times our size. And now we're almost a hundred times the size we were just a decade ago, but I realize that if we think we've got it made, it will be the end of us. We still need to delight our customers with our unique retail service approach to business. We still need to keep our spirit alive with our motivational moments. We need to keep our culture strong and intact. We've got to protect what produced our growth and remember who we are. We're not First National Bank or BigConglomerated Bank. We're Umpqua Bank.

Maintain Your Identity

A big reason growth tends to create problems is that small companies lose sight of who they are as they grow bigger. They try to do too much. Often they grow for growth's sake. In short, they lose their identity. In our case, we say no matter how big we get, we're going to remain a community bank.

There are things that the big national banks do that make a lot of sense—*for them*. But if we were to adopt their ideas or processes, it would take us away from who we are and the strategy we've pursued so successfully.

Umpqua has been operating as a community bank since its inception more than fifty years ago. We started with one bank in 1953, had grown to 6 locations when I got here in 1994, and now have over 125 locations spread across Oregon, southern Washington, and northern California. How can we still say we're a community bank? Because it's our identity and it's the way we still operate: decisions are made locally, our staff is empowered, and we are deeply involved in every community where we have a store.

> Success can do funny things to people, including leaders.

Umpqua is a community bank because we are first and foremost a community of associates empowered to think and act on our customers' behalf. Each associate is given the freedom to consider the specific needs of the local community and take action to fulfill them. Our Universal Associate concept and lack of loan committees enable us to provide faster, more personal service than the national bank down the street. Being a community bank is ingrained in our culture. I don't ever want that to change.

Right now, when investors ask, "What's your strategy going forward?" I tell them, "That's easy—same as it is today." Our strategy as I've described it in this book is simple yet effective. It works well. Of course, that doesn't mean our strategy doesn't get refined and improved—but we are staying the course. We are creating a bank that has regional size and the muscle that goes along with that, and yet operates as a community bank.

We have an opportunity to create what I consider the breakout bank of the Northwest—to create an institution of significance. When I say *significance,* that doesn't necessarily mean size. When analysts look back at this organization in ten to fifteen years to measure our success, they will evaluate the performance of our stock—and that's important. But for me there's another huge element. As a community bank, I believe we have an obligation to give back to the communities we serve. We want to be able to say, "We did pretty well financially, but more important, we affected people's lives in a positive way." And if we can say that, then we did create an institution of significance.

Success can do funny things to people, including leaders. Leaders who have achieved a measure of success in growing their companies can lose touch with the values, methods, and strategies that propelled them on their way. When you do that, you are usually destined for a rude awakening at some point. If you want to keep yourself on a path of sustained growth, remember it's a never-ending journey—and remember who you are.

Growing Big While Staying Small

You know the story about a frog in a kettle of water. Supposedly if you put a frog in a kettle of water at room temperature and gradually turn up the heat, the frog will sit there until it's cooked. The change is so gradual, it doesn't react in time. I'm told that's not really true: even frogs aren't that stupid. Unfortunately, companies can be. The bigger they become, the more processes they develop, the more paperwork and sign-offs they create—and little by little they lose their agility. After a while, they find out they are cooked. Don't get bogged down in the quagmire of size, which will impede future growth.

As their companies get bigger, too many leaders want them to run like well-oiled machines. I think that is really a mistaken desire. When you try to get

> Even frogs aren't that stupid. Unfortunately, companies can be.

your company to operate like a machine, you spend all your time tinkering with processes and machinery—and you often forget to look out the window to see the revolution bearing down on you. At Umpqua, we don't run smoothly all the time, I'll admit that, but we do run quickly—and we keep our eyes on the world outside.

The challenge is to grow but to operate as a smaller, agile, quick-to-react organization. I can't do that if I allow processes to run the company. We have to have *people* looking at each other around the table, deciding what we need to do and then doing it, pulling the trigger. If you are going to grow big and stay agile, you'd better have three things: a sense of urgency, focus, and intensity.

- *A sense of urgency* means that you take action quickly, right away. If you see a problem, you get to work fixing it right away. If you see an opportunity, you move. Of course, sometimes you need to collect data to make a decision, but you do it quickly and then you decide. When you have a decision to make that is troubling you, a good question to ask yourself is, In the big scheme of things, how important is it really? Most of the time, it won't be a bet-the-company issue. Decide and move on.
- *Focus* means you keep your eye on the ball. When you are focused, you know what your strategy is, understand the elements that need to be in place to implement your strategy, and don't get distracted by side issues. I said before that leading for growth isn't rocket science. It's about persistently focusing on the things that will make a difference.
- *Intensity* requires keeping passion alive in yourself and your company. You don't do things half-heartedly. Our culture isn't half-hearted; it's intense. We don't just pay lip service to our values, we believe in them intensely.

Small companies often have a sense of urgency, focus, and intensity because they live close to the edge. These qualities are critical for survival. As companies grow, they can get soft. But keeping your sense of urgency, focus, and intensity alive can give you a tremendous competitive advantage. It's just another reason why paying attention to your culture is so important.

Keep Bureaucracy in Check

Bureaucracy is the enemy of culture. The best way I know of to keep bureaucracy in check is to empower your people to hunt down and eliminate bureaucratic barriers. The people in the trenches are the ones who run into them. The leader doesn't. You're sitting at your desk and everything looks fine and dandy. It's the people in the trenches who come up against processes and procedures and wonder, "Why are we doing this?" Something they could easily do in a minute, for example, may have turned into a two-day process. It's happened to us at Umpqua. Let me tell you a true story.

We had centralized the backroom operations, taking them out of our stores, so our associates only had to deal with customers. This led to a change of address process: when a customer came into one of our stores and had a change of address, the store associate would fill out a form for the customer and send it into the central office to have the change made. And that would take one or two days. Sometimes the people in the central office would input the change wrong, making a typo, forcing local store associates to check for errors. The process was a mess, but it took someone looking at it with fresh eyes to spot it.

I was having a focus group meeting with a group of our new associates from Humboldt Bank, which we had just acquired. And one of the tellers asked me why we had this change of address process. "At Humboldt, when a customer came in with a change of address, the teller would just go into the system and make the change, right then and there. It took a few seconds." She wanted to know what the point was of filling out a form and sending it into the central operations. Of course, I had to admit I didn't know. I surmised that we thought central operations would be more accurate. But it wasn't. That

> The people in the trenches are the ones who run into bureaucratic barriers. The leader doesn't. You're sitting at your desk and everything looks fine and dandy.

one observation from the front lines saved us thousands of dollars and hundreds of hours of unnecessary work. As you can imagine, the process was simplified to the satisfaction of everyone involved. What processes are you following that need to be thrown out?

I discussed our focus groups and Town Hall meetings awhile back. They really do help me and our executives stay in touch with what is happening in the company. But they aren't enough. People need a regular channel to alert us to bureaucratic bottlenecks. If something is bothering someone today, it's not fair to ask them to wait two or three months for the next Town Hall meeting. We have set up an application called PulsePoint on Umpqua's internal Web site, providing an easy online suggestion box for our associates. If they see something going on that doesn't make sense (like filling out a form for a change of address) or is too cumbersome, they let us know. If they have an idea for a better way of doing something, they send it in using PulsePoint. And we pay a reward for those we implement.

I tell people that the primary purpose of PulsePoint is to help us avoid "big bank creep." If you see something that is creating bureaucracy that slows us down, send it in. It's *everyone's* job in the company to ask, Why are we doing this? Does it make sense? Is there a better way, a faster way, an easier way? You've got to empower people to challenge standard operating procedures and then reward them for doing so.

If you don't encourage people to suggest improvements that cut through bureaucratic barriers, a number of things happen, all bad. First, people just keep doing things the old-fashioned way and nothing gets better—you stagnate. Moreover, after dealing with bureaucratic and senseless routines for a while, a lot of people will get frustrated. Many will eventually burn out and quit. Or what is even worse, people get burned out but don't quit; they just put in their time going through the motions. Those people will drive your customers away.

We allow people to tell us what is not working. We keep our lines of communication open.

Stay True to Your Values

The biggest challenge for any growing company is to stay true to the values that put it on a path of growth. Our values are as solid today as they were when we were first starting out. Our core values—

EXHIBIT 21.1   OUR CORE VALUES

These are the heart and soul of who we are as a bank and as people. They represent our commitment to excellence, the way we treat everyone around us, and they remind us why we're here.

Community

Umpqua demonstrates an unsurpassed commitment to the communities we serve by our stewardship, leadership, involvement, protection and expansion of community wealth, sharing our communities' risks, and investing in our communities' future. As the premier community bank, we seek to make a difference in every community we serve. By doing so we are a "community bank" in the truest sense.

People

Umpqua's Associates demonstrate their professional and personal commitment to excellence in everything they do through creative leadership, taking initiative, continuous innovation, creative problem solving, superior service, and providing what customers want. In turn, Associates enjoy participation in a variety of incentive plans, recognition and reward programs, and career opportunities only available in a vibrant, growing organization.

Culture

Our culture is the heart and soul of the Umpqua experience. It is what sets us apart from our competitors and encourages the public to say, "They're different!" Our culture consists of an incredible service and sales environment that our Associates live and breathe, and our customers experience. It's the behavior we exhibit internally and externally that allows us to say, "We're the World's Greatest Bank."

Action

Umpqua acts to provide financial security and opportunity through integrity and honesty, to earn and retain customer trust and confidence, and to always strive to improve already high standards. We seek to provide solutions to meet our customers' needs. We go about our business with an ongoing sense of urgency to insure action and responses that "wow" our customers.

community, people, culture, and action—are shown in Exhibit 21.1 and reflect who we are. I like to think that they are as solid, genuine, and down-to-earth as the people we count as our customers.

As your company grows, don't let complexity crowd out the values and strategies that helped you grow in the first place. Remember who you are.

 MOTIVATIONAL MOMENT

Who Are You?

Give each participant the following list of roles needed for effective teamwork. Have them write the name of a person on their team (including themselves) who best exemplifies each role listed. Once they have completed this, discuss how important it is that all team members assume most of the roles on the list at one time or another.

Leader	Morale Booster
Facilitator	Trailblazer
Motivator	Guide
Team Captain	Teacher
Quarterback	Counselor
Cheerleader	Mentor
Rally Person	Adviser
Trainer	Coach

Chapter 22

Mergers and Acquisitions Done Right

As I pointed out earlier, our strategy has not been to grow through acquisitions. Our strategy was and is to create organic growth. We wouldn't have put the huge focus we have on customer service, marketing, store design, and creating a unique customer experience if our strategy was to grow by acquisitions. But when an acquisition opportunity comes along that makes sense, we will consider it. Acquisitions are really an offshoot, a side benefit, of our success with our core strategy. We've integrated more than a dozen financial institutions into Umpqua over the past decade.

I've saved this discussion of mergers and acquisitions (M&A) for the end of the book, because virtually all the earlier chapters are needed to put two companies together and make an acquisition work. All the points about leadership, empowerment, holding people accountable, explaining your movie, measuring intangibles, enhancing your culture, and all the rest come into play in merging two companies into one. You've got to get them right if you want to ensure that the acquisition strengthens your culture instead of diluting or distorting it. To me, that is the key.

If the people coming on board through an acquisition don't buy into our culture, we're in big trouble. We have one brand, Umpqua Bank, and as I have stressed repeatedly, our culture is a big part of our brand. So we work incredibly hard to win over the new people who come on board.

We have successfully, if not always smoothly, integrated every company we have acquired in a way that maintained and enhanced our unique Umpqua culture. Here's the proof. When we were ranked as the Best Company to Work For in the state of Oregon a few years ago, we had already acquired eleven banks. *Oregon Business,* the magazine that prepared the rankings, based them in large part on employee interviews. They didn't interview me, they interviewed our associates—many of whom came from these eleven different banks—all now working for Umpqua. And these people said we were the best company they've ever worked for.

I am proud of that. If these people, new to Umpqua, can rank us number 1, it says we must have something special. To me, it validates how powerful our culture is.

I'll talk about making M&A decisions and deals later in the chapter. Those are relatively easy. The hard part of a transaction is making sure an acquisition works *once the deal is done.* And that's where a lot of companies fail. The business press is filled with stories of failed acquisitions—full of culture clashes, power struggles, and the like. I am pleased to say that we have avoided those pitfalls.

Successful Integration Strategies

Nothing causes greater uncertainty among employees than learning that the company they work for is going to be acquired. With any M&A deal, you are dealing with people who naturally have a fear of the unknown: "What is going to happen to me?" The leader has to resolve that fear quickly to get the frontline people comfortable with the merger process.

Winning the hearts and minds of our new associates has been at the forefront of every merger effort conducted by Umpqua. We don't wait around for the ink to dry on the contracts. Once a M&A deal is agreed to, it has to be looked at by the regulators and voted on by stockholders before it becomes final. Normally it takes four or five months to close a deal. I've seen a lot of companies wait for the deal to be approved before starting the integration process. Not us. Once we have announced a deal, we start laying the groundwork for integration immediately, so when it does close, we have built three or four months of momentum.

Our top priority during this period: Communicate, communicate, communicate! We don't worry about the executives who may be retiring or stepping aside. We worry about the tellers, loan officers, and other frontline people who deal with customers, because they are the people customers are going to talk to about the deal and ask whether it's a good thing or not. And if the frontline people don't feel good about the merger, customers are going to hear about it and they may take their business someplace else. The *Sacramento Bee* newspaper recently did a story on our acquisition of Western Sierra Bank in northern California. They interviewed a customer of Western Sierra who illustrates why keeping our associates happy throughout the merger process is so important:

> Elk Grove business owner Joseph Piazza expressed optimism about his bank dealings. He started an account for his California Chill Frozen Custard shop 17 months ago at what was then a Western Sierra branch just a few doors down from his store. His biggest concern was that the bank's staff would leave. They haven't. He's staying too.
>
> "It's all about the service," Piazza said. "I don't get the sense that's going to change. It might even get better."

So we work hard to win over the employees of the acquired company and allay their fears. And the only way to do that is communicate often and honestly with them.

Most acquisitions will yield synergies from backroom consolidation and therefore job losses. People will usually know which departments are going to take those losses, and they worry, Do I start looking for a new job now or wait? If they start leaving early, it could jeopardize ongoing operations and the transaction.

So you've got to be very straight with people. We take the position that we are not going to fire people, but we will eliminate positions. It makes a big difference in how people perceive the transaction. For example, we might say, "Your position will be eliminated in three months, but until then, your job is secure. And we will work with you to find another position in the bank as things open up because of normal turnover."

In doing a number of M&A deals, I have discovered that if you deal with people openly and honestly, they can handle it. They can handle the disruption even if you tell them their job is being eliminated in three months. They have time to make plans, and normally will not overreact. But it's up to the leader to make sure it works that way.

By now, I hope you realize we believe in taking care of the people. When we acquired Humboldt Bank in Eureka, a coastal town in northern California that had a struggling economy—fishing was going by the wayside, lumber was declining—we planned to eliminate close to a hundred positions, which could have been devastating to that small community. We realized that, so we created a career center inside one of our facilities for the affected employees and their spouses as well. We offered classes in interview skills, résumé preparation, and business skills—and even provided money for them to buy clothes to use for interviews. Of course we listed all the open positions at Umpqua and invited applications, and set up interviews at the facility and allowed other companies, even other banks, to participate in interviewing these people. Out of the hundred people whose positions were being eliminated, all but six people found other jobs through these efforts. And of those six, two ended up retiring. The effort was very worthwhile and actually helped reinforce our culture.

When we acquire a company, we change the name as quickly as we can, usually within a few weeks. We want the new people to know who they work for—they work for Umpqua. And we want them to follow our standards. We elevate standards of excellence, introduce name badges and provide business cards to all associates, require all to use our telephone greeting, "Thank you for calling the World's Greatest Bank," introduce our Universal Associate concept, and provide the hundreds of hours of training needed to get everyone up to speed.

As we explain our culture and our standards, our expectations do cause some people to retreat into denial or to question what this is all about. We explain our belief in the ability of each associate to make a successful transition to our culture. And we tell them the Umpqua story and explain that along with our high standards we also bring new opportunities such as an expanded line of products, associate empowerment, incentive plans, and many reward and recognition opportunities. In this environment, there are always great stories of success with people really embracing the new culture—and not surprisingly there are other stories of people choosing to pursue their careers elsewhere. And that's okay! You need to try to win people over, but you also have to give them the ability to opt out. We want people who are committed to our vision—who can take pride in our standards of excellence, commitment to community banking, memorable customer service, and associate empowerment—all those things that have enabled us to remain unique.

Making M&A Decisions

If you're going to buy another company, whether it's a bank or a hardware store, you have two hurdles to get over before deciding to do it. The first is the strategic rationale. You need to ask, Why does this make sense for us? If the best reason you can come up with is that you will get bigger, you could be making a big mistake. That is not a strategic rationale. A strategic rationale might be taking out a competitor in the marketplace. It could be bringing in new products that you can't develop on your own. It could introduce you to a new market. An acquisition shouldn't just make you bigger, it should make you *better*.

Our motivation to acquire another bank is never just that it will make us bigger. I want to know, How does it advance our brand? How does it help our footprint? And can it get us there faster than if we opened our own stores one at a time? In my particular business, and probably every business, the strategic rationale is the hardest hurdle to overcome. It's usually not black and white and you have to do some soul-searching.

> An acquisition shouldn't just make you bigger, it should make you *better*.

The second hurdle to get over involves the financial metrics of the transaction. For some companies, it might mean asking, Is the cash flow there? For us, it usually involves asking whether it is good for our shareholders: Is it going to improve earnings per share? Normally the financial metrics are easy enough. You put the numbers in your financial model and it works or doesn't. It's more or less black and white.

Sometimes an acquisition looks great initially, but deeper analysis reveals that it just won't work. Too many companies will fall in love with a deal because of the strategic implications, then force the numbers to make it look like a good deal. That's a big mistake— and it usually comes back to bite them. The first discipline in M&A: don't fall in love with a deal. It's your job as a leader to maintain an objective stance. Jack Welch always looked at a potential deal trying to find out why it would be wrong for GE. That cynical approach is good. The other question you need to ask is, Why are they selling? What is their motivation in seeking to be acquired?

> You have to ask yourself what you are going to look like once the deal is done.

You also have to ask yourself what you are going to look like once the deal is done. Some companies make a big mistake in allowing the acquired company to decide who on its board is going to move over to your board. That will not work. They're not going to pick people based on what your board needs. They're going to pick people based on who they like, who they owe a favor to, and so on. We tell the chairman of the acquired company to find out who is interested in serving on our board and ask them to submit their résumés to our nominating committee, and we will decide who is best for us.

You also have to consider your new shareholders. Are they going to like the deal once it's complete? At the end of the day, all the shareholders you are dealing with on the deal are going to be your shareholders. To me that means I want them happy. If I overpay, say $25 a share for a stock that was worth $20, it may look good to those shareholders in the short run. But if I've overpaid, after the deal closes, my stock might fall by more than $5, wiping out the premium I paid—and then I've got a lot of unhappy campers to deal with.

I always want to give the shareholders of the acquired company an upside, where after a year, the stock is worth more than it was at the point of acquisition. Then they'll be in a position where they made a couple of bucks on the deal right away, due to a reasonable acquisition premium, and then after a year, they can see that they've made another couple of bucks. Then you'll have contented shareholders.

Whether you are selling or buying, you want to pick your partner. Part of my job in doing an acquisition is to convince them that we're the best partner. It should make strategic sense for both companies. Because of that, I don't believe in auctions. Someone who climbs onto the auction block looking for the highest bidder is not thinking about strategic fit. Another reason we never get involved in auctions is that we will *never* be the highest bidder; our strategy of giving shareholders of the acquired company an upside makes that a certainty.

Ultimately, It's All About Our Culture

I think our acquisitions have worked so well because ultimately people learn to appreciate our culture and take pride in being Umpqua associates. We've had banks come to us and say, "We'd like to get together, but the cultural differences between our companies are going to be very difficult to negotiate." I sort of chuckle when I hear that, because they don't understand that the Umpqua culture is a welcoming, nonthreatening, living thing that people really grow to like. Six months or a year after an acquisition, the new associates come to our Celebration of Excellence and get as jazzed up as the people who have been with us ten years. It doesn't take long for them to get it.

MOTIVATIONAL MOMENT

Welcome to Umpqua

This is an exercise we often use after an acquisition to introduce the new associates to our company and our culture. You can readily adapt it to focus on the values your culture embodies.
—*Ray*

Putting Together Umpqua's Culture

Distribute a "Square Me" key chain (the puzzle shown in Figure 22.1) to each of the participants. Tell them to break it apart into separate pieces. They will be asked to pick up only one piece at a time as you talk about what each piece represents. As they accumulate the pieces, they can begin to form a square as you move through the process. (They should only be playing with the pieces you have asked them to pick up; the small square should not be used at this time.)

Piece #1

"We are excited to bring the 'Umpqua look' to you and your customers. This piece of the puzzle represents how different we are from other banks. The look and feel of our stores is unique and our associates are proud of who we are. They offer a warm invitation to customers and encourage them to hang out—and while they're here, we can meet and exceed their every banking need. It's the details that we pay attention to—from the neat, clean look of the countertops and tables, to the creative marketing displays in the lobby—that make us The World's Greatest Bank."

Piece #2

"This piece represents how much we value our Associates. We have various rewards and recognition programs that focus on the day-to-day successes of our associates. We know that you are bringing many talents, skills, and knowledge to the combined company and we believe you should be acknowledged and recognized for your positive contributions."

Piece #3
"This piece represents our focus on creating a memorable experience for each of our customers. We set the bar high and our Quality Service Standards are a written statement of the clear expectations for our associates. Review them—focus on how important it is to pay attention to the details and to continually elevate our standards. We strive for consistency in service for both our internal and external customers."

Piece #4
"Umpqua Bank is a community bank and will remain a community bank no matter how large we become. It's important that we cultivate relationships with our customers, learn their names and faces, and who they really are. We want to remain focused on their needs and continue to be active in the communities we serve. The relationships with your customers will continue to be strong and you will have more resources and tools to make it even better."

At this time, the participants should be able to complete a perfect square with four pieces—if they do not have it, give them a minute or two . . . encourage them to use teamwork, but get them all to make the square.

"But wait a minute . . . there's something missing."

At this point, have the participants pick up the small square. Tell them that all the programs, recognition, community involvement, and innovative store design, do not make us successful without this essential piece.

Piece #5
"The essential piece is represented by this square, and that piece is YOU! So take a few minutes to add 'you' to the puzzle. Take apart your four-piece square, add the essential piece and make a square with all five pieces (Figure 22.2). You'll see that adding 'you' to Umpqua makes our puzzle complete."

FIGURE 22.1   THE SQUARE ME PUZZLE

Available from: Ernest W. Loew Company, 309 Forest Drive, Erie, PA 16505

FIGURE 22.2   SQUARE ME PUZZLE SOLUTIONS

Conclusion

Making Relentless Progress

As I said at the outset, you get better or worse—you cannot stay the same. There is no Door Number Three. Once you know you are going to change and evolve, regardless of what you do, the challenge becomes to guide change so that you get better, not worse. In other words, change is going to happen: Do you want to be in charge of it, or do you want change to be in charge of you? If you want to be the one in charge, get busy.

In this book I have focused on leading for growth—not because getting bigger is the goal, but because *getting better* is. Growth means many different things. On a personal level, it means developing maturity, self-insight, even wisdom. In an organization, it means developing a deeper understanding of your organization and the markets you serve, increasing your bench strength, improving your products and services, and much more.

> Do you want to be in charge of change, or do you want change to be in charge of you? If you want to be the one in charge, get busy.

Every organization has to be committed to the relentless pursuit of progress if it wants to stay vibrant and relevant. I tell my execs that I expect them to make progress every single day. That doesn't mean that I want them to keep plodding ahead in a straight line toward a goal. Making progress is a never-ending journey, one with no finish line. As I see it, people are making progress when they are thinking strategically about the future in everything they do, asking what's around the next corner, what we are going to do next to continue to create value, how we are going to do it, and how it will impact our customers and associates.

Progress does not always mean doggedly staying the course; sometimes it means changing direction. I have had executives come to me and tell me that they decided to delay a new initiative we had discussed, because the timing wasn't right and other initiatives were more important at the time. "That's outstanding," I told them. "You've dug into the details, questioned assumptions, and achieved a deeper understanding of our strategic needs." In other words, they had lifted themselves above the battlefield. To me, that's progress.

My goal in leading Umpqua was never just to make it big. More than size, I have been focused all along on significance. Umpqua is significant: it matters in the lives of the people who work here, in the lives of our customers, and in our communities. We are financially solid, a dependable and trustworthy enterprise that is positioned to continue to grow over the next decades as new leaders take the helm. That is what matters to me, not size.

Believe in Yourself

When you want to accomplish something that really matters—building your company, entering a new market, or fending off a fierce competitor, for example—face the fact that it is never going to be easy. You're going to bleed for it. When you want something really worthwhile, you have to work to get it. You've got to believe in your abilities and the power of your vision or it's not going to happen. You can get battered and bruised, but if you believe—if you have the positive passion I discussed in Chapter Three—you persevere.

You've got to have confidence in your abilities to face the challenges that your vision of the company and its future is going to bring to the table. I explained back in Chapter Three how we started calling ourselves "The World's Greatest Bank." It wasn't a boast but an affirmation of our belief that we could become a great company. I really believed it! I was passionate about it. I'm still passionate about it—and so are all Umpqua associates. Together, we can accomplish anything.

You can't fake your belief in yourself and your vision. Your people, your customers, and your competitors will test you and your commitment daily. As I said earlier, when you are a leader, people watch every move you make, and they want to know if you really are committed. If they sense any hesitation in your words or actions they will not follow you. You've got to believe with a positive passion.

The First Job of a Leader

The first job of a leader, every single day, can be wrapped up in one word: *Persuasion*. As leaders, we need to persuade people to see things our way, to believe in the vision, to put their hearts and souls into the company. We have to persuade customers that we really offer something of distinctive value and the larger community that we are valuable corporate citizens.

I'm not talking about browbeating people into agreeing with you. I'm talking about communicating with people so they can say, "I really get it, I really believe." You do this only partly with words, because actions speak so much louder. What really convinces people is when they see you with their own eyes living out the values you profess. What makes your vision real to others is seeing how relentlessly you pursue it. What makes you persuasive, ultimately, is doing what you say you will do every single day.

Nothing Is Impossible

I have a plaque on my desk; it says "Nothing Is Impossible." That plaque is there to remind me constantly not to get talked out of a good idea; it reminds me that if you have positive passion and discipline, and you empower your people, you and your team can achieve impossible things.

To me impossible goals address things that we want to accomplish that appear to be out of reach for one reason or another. There seem to be too many insurmountable barriers. We have to believe we can accomplish impossible things. The alternative is unacceptable, resigning ourselves to the status quo. Solving world hunger may seem impossible, yet why would anybody want to believe it can't be done? If we don't believe we can accomplish the impossible, innovation and greatness will fall by the wayside and critical problems will never be solved.

> If you lead an organization, you've got the opportunity to create something incredibly special.

At Umpqua, I have always believed we could accomplish the impossible. And we have. In 1994, Umpqua was a $140 million bank with 6 locations in an out-of-the-way corner of rural Oregon—and today we are the largest community bank in the Northwest, spreading across three states, with over 125 locations and $7 billion in assets.

Most people would have thought that to be impossible back in 1994. But we achieved it!

Don't worry if your vision sounds corny, unrealistic, unreasonable, or even impossible. If you lead an organization, you've got the opportunity to create something incredibly special.

So what's stopping you? Get busy.

 MOTIVATIONAL MOMENT

Build a Castle

Tell the following story.

Three bricklayers were asked what they were doing.

The first replied, "I'm laying bricks."

The second said, "I'm earning a living."

But the third said, "I'm building a castle."

Ask: Are you building a castle? Are you laying the foundation for a great company? Go around the room and ask each team member for a brief phrase that personally describes how they contribute to building a great company.

We all have castles to build. Let's get busy!
—*Ray*

Acknowledgments

When I first started on my journey here at Umpqua Bank in 1994 I was totally focused on the mission at hand: determine how to differentiate the bank. Like any other business, we had to find our niche in order to have any chance to grow the organization and create value for our shareholders. Believe me—a book was never considered. Over the years and as the company grew so much was being written about us and our strategy for growth that on Wall Street we were given the tag line of "the never-ending story." Out of one of my trips to New York City I had the opportunity to meet with John Byrne, who at the time was with *Fast Company,* which by the way is a great periodical to read for incredible ideas. From our meeting (where I believe we both got caught up in the passion for what we do), John thought there was an interesting story here that should be told; he introduced me and our company to Neal Maillet of Jossey-Bass/Wiley. The rest is history.

This book has been a labor of love for me over the last year. And I have a lot of people to thank for their assistance with the book and others who have provided encouragement, inspired me to "step out," and supported me over the last ten years.

First and foremost I must acknowledge Alan Shrader, my partner in crime, who endured my rambling rants about the contents of the book. Alan, you are the best; thanks for all the hard work you put into our publication. I also thank all the people at Jossey-Bass who have been involved in the project, including Neal Maillet for the leadership, enthusiasm, and direction you patiently provided a rookie; Mary Garrett and Hilary Powers for the comprehensive editing; Jessie Mandle for the public relations activities; and Carolyn Carlstroem, who has been instrumental in the marketing of the book.

I also wish to acknowledge an incredible group of people who have stood alongside and behind me when needed as the company grew up. First, the board of directors of Umpqua Bank when we started: Milt Herbert, Don Kruse, Neil Hummel, Dick Peterson, Allyn Ford, Lynn Herbert, Bob Hansen, Ron Doan, and Hal Ball. Without you guys this book could not have been written. Then perhaps the most important group of people that I need to acknowledge are those who live the story of Umpqua Bank every day. To all my associates within the company, my heartfelt thanks for trusting me and—as only you know—"giving me the benefit of the doubt." Thanks also go to the company's current board of directors and my executive management team: Lorelei Brennan, Brad Copeland, Dave Edson, Bill Fike, Barbara Baker, Dan Sullivan, Lani Hayward, Gary Neal, Ron Farnsworth, Neal McLaughlin, Mark Tarmy, Steve Philpott, Steve May, and Ric Carey. You have endured a lot from me over the years and you have always answered . . . look what you have built.

I also wish to acknowledge Tom Savinar, a true friend, for his relentless encouragement, his quick wit, and his ability to pull a great bottle of wine out of the cellar at the right time. Tom, thanks for your unbiased advice over the years.

Finally, to my family—Bobbi, Aimee, Kyle, Brook, and Jackson—for their love. And to my parents, thanks for making everything possible. On the date this book is scheduled to be published I will be able to add another name to this list, our second grandchild.

—R. D.

The Authors

Ray Davis is a pioneer of change in the banking industry, revolutionizing how banks look, feel, sound, and operate. As president and CEO of Umpqua Holdings Corporation, parent company of Umpqua Bank, Davis took a small regional bank with six locations and grew it into one of the most innovative and dynamic community banks in the country. Davis has been recognized in numerous national publications, including the *Wall Street Journal,* the *New York Times, Fast Company, BusinessWeek, Business 2.0, Newsweek,* and CNBC. Davis was recently recognized as one of high finance's twenty-five most influential people by *U.S. Banker Magazine.* Davis lives with his wife in Portland, Oregon.

Alan Shrader is a writer and the managing editor of the award-winning journal *Leader to Leader,* published by the Leader to Leader Institute (formerly The Drucker Foundation). He has more than twenty-five years of experience in publishing as an author, editor, director of marketing, and publisher of more than two hundred books on leadership, the social sector, politics, and other topics.

Index

A

Accountability: board role in, of CEO, 124–125; as component of support, 64–67; of manager for employee's actions, 54–55; required to prove sincerity, 28–29, 44–45

Acquisitions. *See* Mergers and acquisitions (M&As); Umpqua Bank acquisitions

Actions: communication to explain, 43–44; as value of Umpqua Bank, 199; vision embodied in, 88–90

Advertising, 18, 153

Apple Computer, 3, 10

Assumptions, looking beyond, 20–21, 22. *See also* Conventional wisdom

AT&T, 88, 141

Attitude, hiring on basis of, 110–111

Authentic Leadership (George), 36

B

Baker, Barbara, 83

Balance, 184–192; celebrations for, 186–188; in communication, 190–191; community involvement for, 189; fun at work for, 184–186, 192; importance of, 184; between short-term results and long-term growth, 191–192; of stakeholder interests, 188

Banana Republic, 142

Banks: lack of creativity in, 12, 142; similarity of, 12–13

Being real, 94–100; being watched and, 94–95; to build brands, 151–153; exercise on, 100; by having fun, 98; personality of leader and, 95–97; by showing emotions, 98–100

Big picture: company losing sight of, 79–80; renaming departments to view, 82–85

Blanchard, Ken, 32

Board of directors, 118–127; with acquisitions, 206; communicating with, 120–121; division of labor between CEO and, 125–126; exercise for, 127; as resource for gaining perspective, 82; responsibilities of members of, 123–124; right people for, 122–123; role in supporting CEO, 124–125; support for, 118–119

Bossidy, Larry, 107–108

Bowerman, Bill, 141

Bowles, Sheldon, 32

Brag Box on Web site, 76

Brands, 150–157; being unique to build, 153–155; being yourself to build, 151–153; defined, 150–151; employees as representatives of, 155–156; exercise on symbols of, 157

Brown, Neal, 32–34, 106–107, 111
Build a Castle exercise, 214
Bureaucracy, 52, 90–91, 197–198
Business: critical questions about, 14; studying, outside your industry, 20. *See also* What business you're in
BusinessWeek, 2, 142, 150, 152, 167–168

C

Carey, Rick, 73
Carlson, Richard, 104
Celebration of Excellence Awards, 36, 186–188
CEO: board role in supporting, 124–125; chairman of board and, 124–125; division of labor between board of directors and, 125–126; getting out in field, 143–144
Chairman of board, 124–125
Change, 40–48; avoiding, of culture, 175–176; being in charge of, 211; exercise on, 48; leading, 46–47; necessity of learning to live with, 1, 41–42; as positive force, 43; rubber band syndrome response to, 40–41; tips on introducing, 42–46
Citigroup, 18
Collins, Jim, 102, 110, 111, 113
Commodities, bank products as, 13
Communication: about change, 43–44; to avoid bureaucracy, 197–198; balance in, 190–191; with board of directors, 120–121; by e-mail vs. phone, 95–96; exercises on, 93, 163–164; to explain actions, 43–44; for integration following acquisition, 202–203; to reinforce culture, 180–181
Communities: connection to, 189; as stakeholders, 188; as value of Umpqua Bank, 133–135, 199
Community bank, Umpqua Bank as, 133–134, 152, 194–195
Compaq, 10, 88
Competition: design for advantage against, 169–170; looking beyond, 20; staying ahead of, 59–60

Concept store. *See* Umpqua Bank concept store (Roseburg, OR)
Conventional wisdom: challenging, 20, 113; exercise on looking beyond, 22; as hindering growth, 11, 21
Cousins, Norman, 30
Creative Strategies Department, 83
Cultural Enhancement Division, 83–84, 179–180
Culture, 175–183; creation of, 181–182; maintenance of, 177–178; where to find, 176–177. *See also* Umpqua Bank culture
Culture Word Search exercise, 182–183
Customer service, 158–164; accountability for funds to improve, 65–66; attention to details for excellent, 104–105; consistency in, 160–162; design and, 168–169; exercise on communication in, 163–164; getting tellers to focus on, 158–161; measuring quality of, 128–133; selling vs., 162–163
Customers, as stakeholders, 188
Cynicism, overcoming, 29

D

Daily Survival Kit exercise, 78
Decisions: giving people permission to make, 65, 69, 75, 76; lack of punishment for, 71–72; on mergers and acquisitions (M&As), 205–207
Design, 165–171; of branches as neighborhood stores, 169–170; for competitive advantage, 169–170; of concept store, 16; customer experience and, 168–169; defined, 166–167; exercise on, 171; importance of, 165–166, 170–171; of Pearl District store, 60–61, 98–99, 168; plants as element of, 106–107; results of attention to, 167–168
Details, attention to, 103–108; for brand protection, 105–107; for excellent

customer service, 104–105; of execution of strategy, 107–108; exercise on, 108; importance of, 103–104

Disagreements, as characteristic of empowered employees, 71

Discipline, 23–29; accountability paired with, 28–29; empowerment with, 73–75; exercise on, 29; motivational moments as element of, 74; passion with, 31; as positive, 28; at Ritz-Carlton, 23–24; spread throughout organization, 26–27; as starting with leader, 24–26

Discover Wall, 170

Disney Company, 105–106, 169

Do the Math exercise, 117

Don't Sweat the Small Stuff—and It's All Small Stuff (Carlson), 104

Drucker, Peter, 21, 133, 134

E

eBay, 2

The Effective Executive (Drucker), 133

E-mail, 95–96

Employees: balance in communication between management and, 190–191; behaviors of empowered, 70–73; "best place to work" selection by, 115, 202; departing, learning truth from, 52; empowerment explained to, 75; environment for truth telling by, 50–52; loyalty to and of, 37–38, 97; making customer service priority of, 158–161, 162; making decisions without asking permission, 65, 71–72, 75, 76; as representatives of brand, 155–156; requiring accountability of, 28–29, 44–45; retail businesses observed by, 15–16, 20, 160–161; selling by, 162–163; as stakeholders, 188; support for, 45, 61; tips on introducing change to, 42–46; training for, 16, 62, 83, 85, 111, 180; trust between leader and, 53–55; Universal Associate conception of, 161–163, 166; volunteer work by, 134, 189

Empowerment, 69–78; behavior characteristic of, 70–73; discipline with, 73–75; example of power of, 76–77; exercise on, 78; rewarding initiative necessary for, 75–76

Enron, 184

Ethics, 135–136

Exceptions, when supporting people, 62–63

Execution: The Discipline of Getting Things Done (Bossidy), 107

F

Fast Company, 2, 82, 142–143, 152

Feedback. *See* What's going on behind your back

Finding revolutions, 141–149; by asking "dumb" questions, 146–147; before they find you, 141; exercise on, 149; by leaving building, 143–144; by looking outside your industry, 142–143, 144–145; by partnering, 145–146; in small differences, 141–142; by taking off blinders, 147–148

Firestone, 135

Firing people. *See* Letting people go

First Impressions exercise, 108

Focus, as characteristic of small agile companies, 196

Focus groups, 45, 90, 197–198

Ford, Allyn, 124

Ford Motor Company, 135

Frohnmayer, David, 41

Fun at work: exercise on, 192; importance of, 5; to maintain balance, 184–186; motivational moments as, 5, 185–186; through laughter, 98

G

Gaining perspective, 79–86; exercise on, 86; methods for, 80–84; paradigm busting for, 85. *See also* Big picture

Gap, 14, 15, 142

General Motors, 88

George, Bill, 36

Gerstner, Lou, 144
Getting to Know You exercise, 100
Giuliani, Rudy, 30
Goals: of growth, 1, 211; impossible, 213–214; unreasonable, 24–25, 35; visions vs., 87
Good to Great (Collins), 110
Google, 2
Growth: balance between short-term results and, 191–192; conventional wisdom as hindering, 11, 21; goal of, 1, 211; maintaining identity with, 193–195; prerequisites for, 7–8; of Umpqua Bank, 2, 214; vision and, 91–93

H
Hamel, Gary, 35, 59
Happy talk, 53, 55–56
Hayward, Lani, 83
Hiring people, 109–117; on basis of attitude and spirit, 110–111; exercise on, 117; motivation for working for organization and, 114–116; as ongoing process, 111–113; with retail background, 15; for Umpqua concept store, 16, 110–111
HSBC, 18
Human being, leaders acting like, 46
Human Spider Web exercise, 86
Humboldt Bank, 154, 197–198, 204
Hunt, Sandy, 94

I
IBM, 10
Identity, 193–200; avoiding bureaucracy as part of, 197–198; exercise on, 200; maintaining, while growing, 193–195; as small agile organization, 195–196; staying true to values and, 198–200
Intangibles, 128–137; ethics as, 135–136; importance of, 128, 136; quality as, 128–133, 137; values as, 133–135. *See also* Culture

Intensity, as characteristic of small agile companies, 196
Is 99.9 Percent Quality Service? exercise, 137

J
Jobs, Steve, 10, 165–166
Johnson & Johnson, 135

K
Kelleher, Herb, 169
Kiel, Fred, 135
Kmart, 88, 141, 170
Knight, Phil, 141
Kodak, 141
Kotter, John, 46
Kruse, Don, 119

L
Lafley, A. G., 146, 166
Leaders: as being constantly watched, 27, 94; cultural role of, 176–177; discipline and, 24–27; happy talk by, 55–56; lack of creativity of, in banking, 12, 142; leading vs. managing change, 46–47; loyalty to employees, 37–38, 97; passion and, 35–38; persuasion as job of, 213; roles of, 57–58; support role of, 61–62; techniques for change introduction by, 42–46; trust between staff and, 53–55. *See also* CEO; Management
Leading Change (Kotter), 46
Leading the Revolution (Hamel), 59
Lennick, Doug, 135
Letting people go: necessity of, 113–114; who manage by intimidation, 53–55; who worked "bankers' hours," 109–110
Levis, Kay, 132
Listening, 45, 52. *See also* Focus groups
Logos: exercise on, 157; proper display of, 103–104
Look Around exercise, 149

Loyalty: to employees, 37–38, 97; of employees, 112–113

M

Make a Face exercise, 163–164
Making decisions. *See* Decisions
Making progress. *See* Progress
Malcolm Baldrige National Quality Award, 23
Management: balance in communication between employees and, 190–191; as at fault for poor customer service, 132; by walking around, 143. *See also* Umpqua Bank managers
Marketing: board member's involvement in, 125–126; handshake, 153; importance of, 5, 139
Marriott, Bill, 143–144
May, Steve, 16, 65, 110, 112
McCallion, Steve, 168
Measurement. *See* Metrics
Medtronic, 36
Mergers and acquisitions (M&As), 201–210; decisions on, 205–207; exercise done after, 208–210; strategies for integration with, 202–205. *See also* Umpqua Bank acquisitions
Metrics: financial, and acquisitions, 205; limitations of, 50; for quality of service, 128–133
Microsoft, 10, 145–146, 167
Mission statement, of Umpqua Bank, 188
Mistakes, lack of punishment for, 71–72
Moral Intelligence (Lennick and Kiel), 135
Motivational moments: about, 5, 74, 185–186; on being real, 100; for board of directors, 127; on change, 48; on communication, 93, 163–164; on culture, 182–183; on design, 171; on details, 108; on discipline, 29; done after acquisitions, 208–210; on empowerment, 78; on finding revolutions, 149; on fun at work, 192; on gaining perspective, 86; on hiring people, 117; on identity, 200; on knowing what's going on, 56; on looking beyond assumptions, 22; on making progress, 214; on passion, 39; on quality, 137, 171; on support, 68; on symbols of brand, 157
Moving Forward exercise, 58

N

Names: of branches as stores, 9; of departments, 82–85; of merged companies, 153, 204; nontraditional, 153
New product launch, technological glitch in, 25–26, 27
Nike, 3, 141
Nordstrom: customer service at, 3; as example of power of empowerment, 76–77; observing and learning from, 15, 20, 161; as place people hang out, 14, 15

O

Optimism, 30. *See also* Passion, positive
Oregon Business magazine, 115, 202

P

Packard, Dave, 5, 139, 165
Paradigm busting, 85
Partnering, 145–146
Passion, positive, 30–39; defined, 30; exercise on, 39; necessity of, 30–31, 212–213; spread throughout organization, 36–38; as starting at top, 35–36; vision as origin of, 32–35
Pay, as motivation for working, 115
Pearl District store. *See* Umpqua Bank Pearl District store
People, as value of Umpqua Bank, 199
Perspective. *See* Gaining perspective

Persuasion, 213
Peters, Tom, 165
Phone, 96, 121
Piazza, Joseph, 203
Plants, in Umpqua Bank stores, 106–107
Play It Loud! exercise, 192
Positive passion. *See* Passion, positive
Power of Communication exercise, 93
President's Club, 179
Procter & Gamble, 146
Progress, 211–214; exercise on, 214; impossible goals and, 213–214; as never-ending process, 211–212; persuasion by leader for, 213; positive passion needed for, 212–213

Q

Quality: exercises on, 137, 171; hotel chain known for, 23; measuring, of service, 128–133
Quality Check exercise, 171

R

Raving Fans (Blanchard and Bowles), 32, 33
Reading, to gain perspective, 82
Reflection, to gain perspective, 80
Restoration Hardware, 15
Retail service business: hiring people with background in, 15; observing examples of, 15–16, 20, 160–161; vision of banks as in, 14–15, 18, 31–32, 59, 142–143, 147
Return on Quality (ROQ) program, 129–133
Revolutions: defined, 141–142; design as, 170. *See also* Finding revolutions
Reward or award programs: Brag Box on Web site, 76; Celebration of Excellence Awards, 36, 186–188; to recognize initiative, 75–76; Return on Quality (ROQ) program, 129–133; Team Recognition Fund, 76
Ritz-Carlton, 3, 23–24, 142, 169

Roseburg store. *See* Umpqua Bank concept store (Roseburg, OR)
Rubber band syndrome: described, 40–41; exercise on, 48; overcoming, 42–46
Rules, empowered employees and, 72–73
Rumblefish, 145

S

Sculley, John, 10
Sears, 88
Self-discipline, 24. *See also* Discipline
Selling, by bank employees, 162–163
Sense of urgency. *See* Urgency, sense of
Shareholders, 188, 206
Shinseki, Eric, 41
Signage, 32–35, 103–104
Significance: as goal, 212; institutions of, 194–195
Simon Says exercise, 29
Slogans, passionate, 32–35
South Umpqua State Bank, 2, 11–12
Southwest Airlines, 2, 169
Staff. *See* Employees
Stakeholders, balancing interests of, 188
Standards: high, 21, 97; unreasonable, 25
Starbucks, 14, 15
Stern, Charlene, 16
Stock analysts, 191–192
Strategic planning retreat, 121
Suppliers, marketing ideas from, 145
Support, 59–68; accountability as component of, 64–67; from board of directors, 118–119, 124–125; exceptions made in, 62–63; exercise on, 68; as key to employee behavior, 61; leader's role in, 37, 61–62; sense of urgency in, 63–64; when introducing change, 45

T

Target, 170–171
Teaching, to gain perspective, 84–85

Team Recognition Fund, 76

Technology, new product launch and, 25–26, 27

Technology Advancement Department, 84

Ten Ways to Get Along Better exercise, 68

Testing, of leader's resolve, 25–26

Thinking "Outside the Boxes" exercise, 22

Thoroughbreds, 113

Titles, 82–85

Town Hall meetings, 36, 64, 90, 198

Toyota, 141

Tradition, pros and cons of, 41

Training, for employees, 16, 62, 83, 85, 111, 180

Trust, between leader and staff, 53–55

Truth, telling: as characteristic of empowerment, 70–71; safe environment for, 50–52, 56

Tylenol tampering crisis, 135

U

Umpqua Bank acquisitions: communication about opting out of, 121; exercise done after, 208–210; of Humboldt Bank, 154, 197–198, 204; ice cream truck to celebrate openings following, 154; integration strategies with, 202–205; retaining focus on vision with, 91–93; success of, 201–202; of Western Sierra Bank, 50–52, 203

Umpqua Bank concept store (Roseburg, OR): designing, 16; hiring and training people for, 16, 110–111; initial reaction to, 16–17; plants at, 106–107; slogan and, 32–34; success of, 18

Umpqua Bank culture: acquisitions and, 204–205, 207; communication to reinforce, 180–181; exercises on, 182–183, 208–210; HR's role to enhance and maintain, 83–84, 179–180; as intangible asset, 19, 128, 175; motivational moments as element of, 185; as providing safety for telling truth, 51–52; role models of, 179; as value of Umpqua Bank, 199

Umpqua Bank managers: created "Customer of the Month" program, 76; with drive-up window problem, 66–67, 90; hired contractor to stripe parking lot, 73; overlooked backward signage, 103–104; rehiring procedure for, 112

Umpqua Bank Pearl District store: design of, 60–61, 98–99, 168; "Friday Nite Flicks" program at, 153

United Airlines, 141

Universal Associates, 161–163, 166

Unreasonable, perception of being, 24–25, 31, 35

Urgency, sense of: as characteristic of small agile companies, 196; as element of leader's personality, 95–97; needed to maintain culture, 177–178; in supporting people, 63–64

U.S. Banker, 142

V

Values: core, of Umpqua Bank, 199; importance of acting on, 133–135; staying true to, 198–200

Vance, Mike, 105–106

Victoria's Secret, 142

Visions, 87–93; actions as embodying, 88–90; of bank as in retail service business, 14–15, 18, 31–32, 59, 142–143, 147; directors' agreement with, 122; goals vs., 87; growth and, 91–93; leader's job of explaining, 87–88; maintaining freshness of, 90–91; as origin of passion, 32–35

Vital Few vs. Trivial Many exercise, 127

Volunteer work, 134, 189

W

Wal-Mart, 79–80, 171

Wall Street Journal, 152

Welch, Jack, 144, 206
Welcome to Umpqua exercise, 208–210
Western Sierra Bank, 50–52, 203
What business you're in: exercise on, 22; figuring out, 19–21; lack of understanding of, 10
What's going on behind your back, 49–56; environment for telling truth about, 50–52, 57; exercise on, 56; happy talk and, 53, 55–56; need to know, 49–50; trust between leader and staff and, 53–55
What's in Your Briefcase? exercise, 39
What's on Your Back? exercise, 56
Who Are You? exercise, 200
World's Greatest Bank University, 36–37, 83, 85, 180

Z
Ziba Design, 60–61, 98–99, 168